Leo Daly

James Joyce
and the Mullingar Connection

with an Introduction by Bernard Share

DE A Dolmen Edition
Published in North America by Humanities Press Inc.

© Leo Daly, 1975
Printed in the Republic of Ireland
ISBN 0 85105 259 2 THE DOLMEN PRESS
ISBN 0 391 00418 2 HUMANITIES PRESS INC.

Bibliography: p.
1. Joyce, James, 1882-1941 — Homes and haunts —
Mullingar, Ire. 2. Joyce, James, 1882-1941.
The portrait of the artist as a young man. I. Title.
PR6019.09Z5284   823'.9'12 [B] 75-33337.

828
J89zd

70-2017

Contents

Bibliographical Note *page* 5

Acknowledgements 6

Introduction 7

An Muileann Cearr ... Mollingar ... Mullingar 9

Stephen Hero in Mullingar 21

Milly Bloom and the photographer's shop 53

A Brilliant Career 57

Epilogue 59

Bibliographical Note

References to the various works of James Joyce as quoted in the following texts relate to:

STEPHEN HERO
The revised edition, with additional material and a Foreword by John J. Slocum and Herbert Cahoon. (Jonathan Cape, London, 1956.) The relevant pages are pp. 240-253.
'Five more pages of James Joyce's *Stephen Hero*.' Edited by J. J. Slocum and H. Cahoon in M. Magalaner (ed.), *A James Joyce Miscellany, second series*. Edited by M. Magalaner. Carbondale, Southern Illinois University Press, 1959.

ULYSSES
The Bodley Head, London, 1937. The Penguin Modern Classics edition (1968 reprint) contains a page concordance with this edition.

FINNEGANS WAKE
Faber and Faber, London, 1939.

A PORTRAIT OF THE ARTIST AS A YOUNG MAN
Jonathan Cape, 1954.

The references to Ellmann refer to Richard Ellmann, *James Joyce*. Oxford University Press, 1959.

Acknowledgements

To Bernard Share and William Bolger, who, so the story goes, discovered this epiphany in my possession one night in the Club at Mullingar, and drew my attention to its possibilities.

To the decent people and shopkeepers of the town of Mullingar who answered countless queries and provided much vital detail.

To the Management of *The Greville Arms Hotel*.

To Alec and Beatrice Reid who offered me the hospitality of their home.

To the staff of *The Westmeath Examiner*, and especially to its Editor, Mr. Nicholas Nally.

To Mr. W. Smith and Miss Marian Keaney of *The Longford-Westmeath Library* who, with their staff offered every assistance. Also the Westmeath Co. Council Staff who helped in many ways.

To Mr. Michael O'Neill and Miss Mary Murphy, Librarian and Archivist of *Radio Telefís Eireann*.

To the Librarians and Staffs of:
  The National Library of Ireland, Dublin;
  The British Museum Newspaper Library at Colindale, London;
  The Central Catholic Library, Dublin.

To Most Rev. Dr. McCormack, Bishop of Meath, and the Cathedral Archivists, Very Rev. Fr. J. Dermody and Rev. P. J. Regan, C.C., and Mr. Philip Mulally, Sacristan, I would offer my sincere thanks.

Acknowledgement also goes to: The Joyce Estate and Messrs. Jonathan Cape, London, for permission to reproduce Joyce's works, and to the Oxford University Press and Richard Ellmann for allowing me to quote from the latter's *James Joyce*.

Lastly to my family, my gratitude belongs, as it must, for reasons which we all know, but rarely see in print.

Introduction

The town of Mullingar has not hitherto featured with any degree of prominence in the multiplicity of meticulously-annotated guidebooks to Joyce's country. Yet here is a book which, without any necessity for over-inflation of the evidence or for special pleading, establishes a positive landmark, a new triangulation point on the Joycean landscape so far beyond the Pale as to have remained, apparently, barely discernible to the critical eye. To grasp the full import of Mr. Daly's undertaking it is only necessary to consider the possibilities of engaging in the same kind of patient archaeology on the site of any other peripheral Joycean locus. Cork? A few equivocal and unamplified references. Zürich? Paris? No: Mullingar remains the one identifiable agglomeration outside the city of Dublin and environs which can lay claim to have provided a significant element of the Joycean sub-culture. One can only regret that the possibility of a full assessment of this significance perished with the rest of *Stephen Hero* in the flames.

Why Mullingar? It is a legitimate question, even — I suspect — to a Mullingar man. The surface explanation, as Mr. Daly points out, is to be found in the facts of Joyce's life at the time, and the concomitant fact that, like many a shrewd artist before and after him, he was ready to feed all kinds of grist to his mill. But the mill, in this case, ground little and small before it stopped — clogged, perhaps, by the unfamiliar texture; and the question of why it stopped is perhaps even more fascinating than why it ever started. *Stephen Hero* offers us a tantalising glimpse of what Joyce did with his Mullingar material — which was almost nothing at all. Apart from the odd germ that was to develop into mature epiphany, he was as near to being a straight reporter of the Midland scene as the Editor of the *Westmeath Examiner*. That virtually all this material disappeared from the final draft of *A Portrait* is in itself interesting, but not really remarkable. Behind this judicious piece of editing there remains, however, the larger question: did Joyce, in Mullingar, come up against something he was not prepared to know about? Was he, in fact, afraid of knowing too much?

More than one critic has remarked that Joyce's Dublin is a severely edited account of that city, and edited, moreover, by a ruthless and biased observer. 'Whole aspects of his native city,' says John Gross, '— social, economic, cultural, architectural — are either ignored or played down and in any case, Dublin isn't Ireland.' Such editing is a perfectly legitimate, one might say mandatory, artistic method — but it provides a key to the Mullingar file. Joyce took care to preserve his vision of Dublin by staying well away from it. In the same way he may have taken an early decision to stay away from the rest of Ireland, both physically and empathetically, in order to preserve the necessary and formative illusion of Dublin as the centre of Ireland, shifting that centre bodily from its traditional location a few miles from the shores of Lough Ennell. Ireland, it is not unfair to say, is seen throughout Joyce's work in strictly Dublin terms, filtered through the mocking, non-Gaelic self-awareness of the urban dweller, Stephen/Bloom/Earwicker. A shift in locus, of the kind beginning to manifest itself in the few salvaged pages of *Stephen Hero*, would have demanded a shift in viewpoint little short of revolutionary in terms of the Joycean universe. Can one now conceive of a Leopold Bloom, canvasser of advertisements for the *Westmeath Examiner*; a daughter gone to the big bad city, cuckolded by the young Mr. Garvey with whom he drinks in the *Greville Arms*, teaming up with a rustic Ur-Stephen to follow a course of provincial depravity culminating in a 'saturnalia of immorality' in the mental hospital? From what we know of Joyce's artistic method the decision to reject the Mullingar material — and the possibility of more Mullingar material — was most likely to have been a careful and considered one. And the residue drops into the void almost without an echo.

The few echoes are not, however, without their own complexities. There is young Milly, sent off on the Midland and Great Western to stand in for the Stephen that might have been; and there is that frontier post on the rim of the commodious vicus of the recirculation itself, the Mullingar House — a hostelry of labyrinthine perplexity, the ramifications of which we will have nothing to do with here beyond observing that it was, at the very least, an interesting choice, given all the pubs on all the roads that emanate from Dublin.

So there we have — and must leave Mullingar: an oasis, or perhaps the mirage of an oasis, in an urban desert, accidentally stumbled upon, perhaps a little more accidentally foresaken. Joyce was, and remained, a city dweller: his pastoral landscapes, even the lyrical Anna Livia passages, have the air of being written by a man who, confronted by a well-dunged pasture, would always put a foot wrong. I know another man, a genuine gravel-voiced Dublin man, for whom anything beyond South King Street is Injun territory. He was once persuaded to take a holiday in the remote fastnesses of Sandymount, only to return in three days with the news that they overcharged you something shockin' for ice-cream (an unlikely story knowing your man) out there. The truth was, of course, simpler: the despised culchies had turned out to be decidedly and disturbingly human.

If any message emerges from Mr. Daly's compendious and fascinating researches it is perhaps no more complicated — and no more simple than that.

BERNARD SHARE

An Muileann Cearr ... Mollingar ... Mullingar

In the Spring of 1880, a labouring man, while digging in the neighbourhood of Mullingar, found what he thought was a metal stamp for making butter prints. He brought the article to a local tradesman, who purchased it for one shilling and sixpence. The tradesman sold it for seven and sixpence to a commercial traveller, from whom it was subsequently purchased at a very enhanced price by Mr. Robert Day, J.P., M.R.I.A., Cork, who has one of the most valuable private collections of antiquities in Ireland. The seal was exhibited by Mr. Day at the Irish National Exhibition of 1882, and attracted great attention, being one of the best preserved of the Ancient Corporate seals of Ireland. It belonged to the Corporation which was established in Anglo-Norman times, when Mullingar was an important town of the Pale. The Corporation was dissolved in 1661 by Charles II when all the Corporate lands comprising, according to the 'Down Survey' ('Lyons's Estates Forfeited in Westmeath'), four lots, amounting in all to 464 acres, were confiscated and granted to Sir Arthur Forbes, ancestor of the present Earl of Granard.

The seal is $2\frac{1}{4}$ inches in diameter, and is made of bronze, with a flange-like handle at the back. In the centre is a mill-wheel within an archway, which, no doubt, represents the mill from which Mullingar derives its name. Over the archway is a heckle emblematic of the flax and woollen industries, for which Mullingar was famous in by-gone times. On the left is a tower, from which springs a demi-Griffin, rampant. (The Griffin formed part of the arms of the Petits, who were Barons of Mullingar.) The meaning of the spire and tented field, with flag flying on the right, has not been determined. Around the seal are the words 'Sigillium Commune de Mollingar'. It is probably fifteenth century work.

Extract from *Annals of Westmeath*

10 | *An Muileann Cearr — Mollingar — Mullingar*

Some of James Joyce's 'Mongolian types' in Mullingar for a day's shopping. Shawls were worn extensively in rural areas well into the 1920's. Three doors above the butcher's shop on the left is the photographer's shop, now a newsagent's, where Milly Bloom was apprenticed.

In the summer of 1898 James Joyce left Belvedere College and entered university. His father had tried to persuade the brilliant student on different courses, but 'some mysterious urges within the boy' warned him against joining the Jesuit Order, joining the staff of Guinness's brewery, reading for the Bar, or becoming a journalist. He recorded his feelings of this happy escape years later:

> So he had passed beyond the challenge of the sentries who had stood as guardians of his boyhood and had sought to keep him among them that he might be subject to them and serve their ends.
> (*A Portrait*, Chapter IV, pp. 187-188)

The same eventful year marked the liberation of his father, John Stanislaus Joyce, from his job in the office of the Collector General of Rates on a hardly adequate pension. This relief aggravated the already unhappy financial circumstances of the parent who for some years had been on the slippery slope. John Joyce had filled his house with bills and debts — four boys and six girls — not to mention eleven mortgages and bankruptcy. His downfall is described vividly, if cruelly, by Stephen in *A Portrait of the Artist,* p. 274:

> A medical student, an oarsman, a tenor, an amateur actor, a shouting politician, a small landlord, a small investor, a drinker, a good fellow, a story teller, somebody's secretary, something in a distillery, a taxgatherer, a bankrupt, and at present a praiser of his own past.

In May 1900 Joyce invited his father to go with him to London where they visited theatres, music halls, and paid some official calls. After a hectic holiday they returned to Ireland in good spirits, with two pence left out of the twelve guineas received earlier by James Joyce for his article on Ibsen in the *Fortnightly Review*.

In the following month John Stanislaus Joyce was given what Slocum and Cahoon in their preface to the revised edition of *Stephen Hero* describe as the task of 'straightening out the confused Mullingar election lists', and he went there at once accompanied by James and other members of the family.

12 | *An Muileann Cearr — Mollingar — Mullingar*

An Muileann Cearr — Mollingar — Mullingar

Two conspicuous tokens has Lann,
Beyond every shrouded cemetery,
A lefthandwise-moving mill for grinding,
And a cloak around its staff.

This quatrain is taken from chapter 97 of a twelfth-century *Life of Saint Colman of Lynn*, which is now preserved in a single manuscript in the town library at Rennes in Brittany, and was published by the Royal Irish Academy under the editorship of Kuno Meyer in 1911. The lefthandwise-moving mill, *An Muileann Cearr*, is the earliest reference to Mullingar to be found. The legend of the reverse mill and how it was so called is given here in Kuno Meyer's translation of *Betha Colmáin Maic Lúachán*.

55. Again, upon a certain time the steward of Conall son of Suibne came to Luachan to demand victuals of him. And Luachan had but one sieve of barley-seed; and he said: "We have not got what you demand of him." But the steward said that they would all be put into the sea or fire unless they found three hundred wheaten cakes with their condiment of butter and milk. And Colman said: "It is permitted to thee to be swallowed up by the earth!" And forthwith the earth swallowed the steward as he went towards his lord to stir him up against Colman, so that ever since hounds have been . . . ing on his head. And when he saw that he began to flee, and [dread] seized all the people; and they said: "Woe to him who shall consume thy food, Colman; and 'tis not we who shall consume it." And for a long time afterwards it was a form of cursing one another among them, viz. "May the death of Cú Mend carry thee off!" as the earth swallowed Loegaire when he was disobedient to Patrick.

56. However, his mother said to Colman: "My good son, help us, for we are in a great plight." Colman went to the mill with his sack upon him, as Colum Cille took the sack upon him to the stone which is in the refectory at Iona (Maelblatha is its name, and there is luck upon every food that is upon it). Now on his arrival there was Conall's corn under the mill and it was wheat. Colman ordered it to cease, for he was in great haste (?); but the steward would not do it at his bidding. "Then put it in," said the cleric, "and we will put (ours in) on this side, and God will divide for us." They did thus, and Colman put his hand against the mill and turned it lefthandwise, so that thenceforward it has been *Mullingar* (*Wry Mill*). And God exchanged the corn so that Colman had wheat and the steward barley. So God's name and Colman's were magnified through the miracle.

* * *

Dominick Street, Mullingar, which was once called Linen Street on account of the number of weavers who lived there. At the right-hand corner Kate O'Neill sells fruit at her stand. Farther up the street Sam Galway's clock hangs from the wall of a small shop. In later years this shop gained the unique reputation of being the only shop in Ireland where 'a Woodbine, a match, and the time, could be purchased for a halfpenny'.

Sterne Street, known also as Jail Street, Mount Street, and now called Seery Street in memory of Brian Seery who was hanged in the 1840's for an assault on the person of Sir Francis Hopkins, Bart. The chief evidence offered by the crown against Seery was, that a cap found at the scene of the crime fitted him!

14 | *An Muileann Cearr — Mollingar — Mullingar*

An Muileann Cearr — Mollingar — Mullingar

A Parnellite meeting in Mullingar in the 1890's. James Joyce mentions in *Stephen Hero* that he found Mullingar people with an 'un-Christian belligerence towards England'. (Ellmann, *James Joyce*, p. 81.)

'Mounting the Guard' at Mullingar Barracks, now called Columb Barracks. James Joyce may have visited here, but as related in *Stephen Hero*, 'Stephen always looked his enemy in the face'; especially the 'two scrupulous lieutenants'. (*Stephen Hero*, p. 244). This photograph was taken *circa* 1900.

96. Now weakness came to Colman son of Luachan, and when the end of his life was appointed for him, his clerics and his monks came to him and wept bitterly in his presence, and begged him to allow them to open the earth on his holy relics, that they might be kept among them in an adorned shrine like (the relics of) every other great saint and chief apostle throughout Ireland. Then Colman granted that, so that it might be a comfort of grief to them, and that his relics might be a halidom against every visible and invisible danger.

97. However, when he had rested three years in the earth, then Fursa the Devout happened to go upon a round throughout Ireland from church to church. Now when he came to Ath in Daire, the bellringer of Lann was striking its bell. "Disgrace of bell-ringing upon thy successor!" said Fursa. "We dare not say anything worse to thee." Then Fursa sat down at Cross Fursa, looking at the wry mill (Mullingar) eastward. 'Tis then he spoke the quatrain:

"Two conspicuous tokens has Lann beyond every shrouded cemetery: a wry mill for grinding, and a cloak around its staff."

Forthwith there came to them the common cowherd of Lann, and bids them welcome, and carries the news (of their arrival) to the erenagh Cuanu son of Cummaine.

In 1540 we read in a description of the Dominican Priory of Mullingar:

There is a water-mill which some way was pledged by the friars to one Gerald Pettyt of Irysshton, gentleman, for 12 marks, value 20 shillings. This mill had been occupied for a year and more, and is still occupied by the said Gerald who asserts that it is his own right and inheritance and was formerly leased by himself to the Friars, who had no other right to it.

The mill referred to was known as the Friars Mill, traditionally said to be the site of the original Muileann Cearr of St. Colman.

Sir Henry Piers in his *Description of the County of Westmeath*, written in 1682 remarks:

The name of this town, Mullingar, if Englished imports the "short mill" — indeed in my time, here hath been an overshaft mill of the least wheel that ever I saw, which with buckets and all was not eight foot in diameter, but now is converted into a breast mill. There are also in this town on the same water (the River Brosna) two other mills.

Friars Mill was still in existence in the nineteenth century, and was held on lease by James Daly from the Royal Canal Company for ninety-nine years from 1822, subject to rent of £24. The mill was sold in the 1860's, became derelict, and was later demolished. The stone and materials of Friars Mill were incorporated into the waterworks station which was built on the site. The old mill wheel was buried here.

A note in the *Gazetteer of Ireland* of 1843 is of interest. Mr. Brewer said:

> We must not conclude our notice of this town without offering some remarks on the old and well known saying — "When the King comes to Mullingar", a circumstance believed, according to the meaning of the saying, to be so improbable, that any boon may be safely promised, the performance of which depends on the actual occurrence of a royal visit. This mode of expressing a thing improbable has grown into very general use in the town and has even been adopted as a legal method of stating a contingency. Thus, several leases of land and houses are granted in supposed actual perpetuity; that is until the King should come to Mullingar. . . .
>
> By some persons it is said that, previous to the Battle at the Boyne, the Catholic inhabitants of Mullingar boasted that, if James succeeded, he would, on arrival at this town, withdraw the Corporation's franchise from the Protestants, and vest the same in Catholic freemen. When William III prevailed, the Protestants retaliated on their disappointed neighbours and tauntingly rebuked any extravagant expectation by remarking, that probably such an anticipated event might take place — "when the King should come to Mullingar".

Contemporary sources in the year 1900, the date at which John Joyce and his family moved to Mullingar, describe the town as the county and assize town of Westmeath, situated in the centre of Ireland on the River Brosna and half encircled by the Royal Canal. The county gaol and courthouses are described as 'substantial, plain buildings', and as well as the Roman Catholic cathedral and the Protestant church, there were Presbyterian and Wesleyan meeting-houses, two convent schools, a Roman Catholic college, a Protestant parochial national school, a county infirmary, extensive infantry barracks, union workhouse, and the lunatic asylum for the counties of Meath, Westmeath and Longford. A post office had been recently erected in the centre of the town at a cost of £2,000. (*Thom's Directory*, 1894).

The Local Government Act of 1898 transferred local power from Protestant land-owners (grand juries and borough councillors) to the Catholic middle-class. The Act specifically excluded clerics from membership of local bodies, and objections were expressed by the clergy because of this discrimination. To facilitate the implementation of the Act, the former parliamentary lists had to be revised and made suitable for elections under the new system. Every polling district had to be split into units, and in cases where the unit had to be subdivided, separate lists had to be compiled for each sub-division. It was on this work of preparing the new lists and straightening out the confusion of the polling districts that John Joyce was employed. He seemed to have had a talent and reputation for this work, and had made a remarkably correct forecast in the General Election of 5 April 1880, when both the candidates he supported were elected against the odds. (See Ellmann, *James Joyce*, pp. 15-16.)

At the Municipal Elections in Mullingar in January, 1900, out of a register of 570 voters, only 175 recorded their votes. The town was blamed for its apathy and for being much behind the times in matters of public improvement. Whole districts had abstained from voting altogether. It was feared that the situation might worsen, as many small occupiers would be disenfranchised owing to the delay in paying rates. 'A Franchise Act was ready to save the votes of Yeomen who went to assist in the war,' the Nationalist Press stressed, 'but there will be no saving of the votes of the unfortunate people disenfranchised through British mismanagement and juggling with Irish affairs.'

In this atmosphere of confusion and speculation, the town prepared for a general election as James Joyce's father prepared the voters' list.

The name 'Bannon' carved on a tree in Portloman Churchyard, on the shores of Lough Owel.

17 | *An Muileann Cearr — Mollingar — Mullingar*

A group of ecclesiastical buildings in Mullingar as they appeared at the turn of the century. On the extreme left is seen the Loreto Convent; in the foreground St. Mary's Christian Brothers' School, and the 'old' Cathedral; between them the Presbytery, or as it was always called 'The Palace'. The new Cathedral of Christ the King replaced the old in the mid 1930's.

Confraternity group taken in 1888. Dan the jarvey, fourth figure (standing) from the left, may well be Dan who drove Stephen in the green trap.

Outside the hotel stands the 'Greville Arms Bus'. Down this street on a sultry July morning, Nash and Garvey of *Stephen Hero* accompanied the author, James Joyce. Farther on, near the Dublin bridge, the body was taken from the Royal Canal.

A *Mullingar District Lunatic Asylum* nurse of the 1900's, maybe one of those criticised by the townspeople for 'traipsing about with every Tom, Dick and Harry of a doctor', instead of minding their patients.

19 | An Muileann Cearr — Mollingar — Mullingar

Belvedere House, Mullingar. This house was built by Robert Rochfort, first Earl of Belvedere in the mid-eighteenth century, and has undergone some changes and alterations since. The terraces, as can be seen from the photograph, are recent additions. Nearby stands the 'Jealous Wall', effectively obstructing the view of Rochfort, once the residence of George Rochfort, who built Belvedere House in Dublin, later Belvedere College.

The entrance arch and gatelodge of Knockdrin Castle. During James Joyce's stay in Mullingar the Castle was occupied by Mr. James, the owner of the first registered motor-vehicle in Mullingar. The ladies are dressed in the recommended cycling attire of those days.

Stephen Hero in Mullingar

Prologue
What follows should be regarded not as a local interpretation of a section of *Stephen Hero* but as a portrait of the town of Mullingar and its surroundings as revealed by James Joyce during his visits there in the years 1900 - 01.

The influence of the Mullingar experience on the writings of Joyce may be of much greater significance than is generally admitted. Only when the existing local political and social background of those years is examined in conjunction with the author's works can a real assessment be made and its importance evaluated.

The connection was two-staged; the immediate one which shaped the 'additional pages' or 'Mullingar' section of *Stephen Hero* and to a lesser extent *A Portrait of the Artist as a Young Man,* and the second or recollective stage which is carried on into *Ulysses* and *Finnegans Wake*. There are many other isolated fragments, some surviving, which belong to those years.

Apart from the well-known connections of Milly Bloom, who worked in the photographer's shop in Mullingar, and the other characters who hail from the neighbourhood, there are also the recurring memories of Bloom and Stephen as they recall the Midlands. These memories are usually expressed as nostalgic reveries — the canal trip on the 'Bugabu' — the famous old boat of the Royal Canal, the many concerns expressed about Milly's welfare, or Stephen just wondering what the weather was like down in Westmeath. The comments might be best described as a series of 'asides'; the word being used in the theatrical sense. At times the recording is free and not synchronized to the Joyce text in theme or time. This vacillation may be excusable if we accept that Joyce's time-tables were adapted to suit his own demands and often bear little relation to a particular or even a realistic chronology.

It is not the purpose of this study to discuss that particular aspect further; rather, hopefully, it offers a series of portraits, of events, of places, and of situations, in the manner of a kaleidoscopic panorama. Variety there certainly is, although some of the colours or forms may hardly qualify as beautiful.

Occasionally the 'connection' may consist of but one single thread in a complex tapestry; again, that which is offered may be a complete and unmistakable pattern. Yet, however faint or nebulous the images, one can but hope that they are at least visible to the viewer; also, that the 'asides' are at all times audible to the listener.

STEPHEN HERO

Cape, 240]

From the Broadstone to Mullingar is a journey of some fifty miles across the midlands of Ireland. Mullingar, the chief town of Westmeath, is the midland capital and there is a great traffic of peasants and cattle between it and Dublin. This fifty-mile journey is made by the train in about two hours and you are therefore to conceive Stephen Daedalus packed in the corner of a third-class carriage and contributing the thin fumes of his cigarettes to the already reeking atmosphere. The carriage was inhabited by a company of peasants nearly every one of whom had a bundle tied in a spotted handkerchief. The carriage smelt strongly of peasants (an odour the debasing humanity of which Stephen remembered to have perceived in the little chapel of Clongowes on the morning of his first communion) and indeed so pungently that the youth could not decide whether he found the odour of sweat [unpleasant] offensive because the peasant sweat is monstrous or because it did not now proceed from his own body. He was not ashamed to admit to himself that he found it [unpleasant] offensive for both of these reasons. The peasants played with blackened edgeless cards from Broadstone onward and whenever it was time for a peasant to leave the company he took up his bundle and went out heavily through the door of the carriage, never closing it behind him. The peasants spoke little and rarely looked at the scene they passed but [at] when they came to Maynooth

Cape, 240] Broadstone Railway Station, affectionately located by West of Ireland travellers as 'seven minutes walk from the Pillar' was in the year 1900, and for many years after, the Dublin terminus for passenger traffic on the Midland Great Western Railway. It eventually became a bus depot, and the rail passenger traffic was shared between Amiens Street and Westland Row, now renamed Connolly and Pearse Stations. There were morning and evening passenger trains serving Galway and Sligo, and the fare to Mullingar was, according to Mr. Bloom in *Ulysses*, p. 588, 'five and six, there and back', third class, naturally! The journey usually took about two hours, often a little more, but seldom less.

Timetable for 2 June 1900
Mullingar to Dublin: 9.10 a.m. 9.20 a.m. 12.55 p.m. 1.10 p.m. 3.10 p.m. 7.20 p.m.
Dublin to Mullingar: 9.15 a.m. 11.50 a.m. 3.30 p.m. 4.40 p.m. 6.15 p.m. night mail 8.20 p.m.
Sunday Train 9 a.m.

The constant 'great traffic' of peasants and cattle mentioned by Joyce was a fact. On fair-days as many as nine specials, each carrying four or five hundred beasts each, left Mullingar. Travelling cattle-jobbers and 'horse-blockers' kept the carriages overcrowded on other days too; the motley companions patiently endured by Stephen on his journey from Broadstone. His first impressions of his fellow travellers are olfactory; the reeking atmosphere and the debasing odour of sweating humanity assailing his sensitive nostrils. The immediate smells seem more pungent than the recollected ones, but he decides that past and present experiences are offensive.

His own contribution to the polluted air, the 'thin fumes of his cigarettes' does not worry him, and it is interesting to note that no mention is made of any other smoker in the carriage or if it is a 'no smoking' compartment.

As Stephen considers his proposed mortifications in *A Portrait*, p. 171, he again makes a special if slightly modified reference to his own olfactory sensitivities:

> ... To mortify his smell was more difficult as he found in himself no instinctive repugnance to bad odours whether they were the odours of the outdoor world, such as those of dung or tar, or the odours of his own person among which he had made many curious comparisons and experiments. ...

The presence of his own 'neat little valise' on the overhead rack, although not as yet mentioned, probably heightens his interest in the 'spotted handkerchiefs' which hold the peasants' belongings. Likewise his minute observations of the scene contrast greatly with the lack of interest generally displayed by his fellow-travellers.

Card-playing was one of the most popular pastimes of the peasants, almost to the extent that the 'blackened edgeless' cards were considered a curse and their use a disease, especially when drink was introduced at all-night sessions.

Report, 25 November 1899, The Westmeath Guardian

> A fair indication of the amount of business done at a recent Mullingar fair is the railway returns and these we have secured through the kindness of Mr. Scollens, Stationmaster, Mullingar. The statistics show that 380 wagons and 50 horse boxes were required for the transit of stock, showing an increase of 21 wagons and 10 horse boxes on the previous November fair. The demand for horse boxes was very keen as a large number of animals of superior quality changed hands.

STEPHEN HERO

Cape, 241]
Station a gentleman dressed in a frock-coat and tall hat who was giving loud directions to a porter concerning a case of machines attracted their wondering attention for several minutes.

At Mullingar Stephen took his neat little valise down from the rack and descended to the platform. When he had passed through the claws

ms. 479]
of the ticket-collectors he paused for a few moments in indecision before he was sighted by the driver of a small dark-green trap. The driver asked was he the young gentleman for Mr. Fulham and on Stephen's answering 'yes' invited him to climb up beside him on the seat. So they set off easily. The trap which was not very clean [and it] jolted a good deal and Stephen looked once or twice anxiously at his oscillating valise but the driver said he need have no fear. The driver when he had said this a few times in the same words fell silent a while and then asked didn't Stephen come from Dublin. Re-assured on this point he fell silent again[st] and began [to] with a deliberate whip to flick flies off the ill-groomed hide between the shafts.

The trap went up the long crooked main street of the town and crossing over the bridge of the canal made out for the country. Stephen remarked that the houses were very small but catching sight of a large square building that stood in grounds closely walled [he asked]

Cape, 241]
Any gentleman with 'a frock-coat and tall hat' attracted peasant attention in the 1900's, and not always for the same reason. The particular gentleman mentioned here, like his 'case of machines', remains unidentified. On his arrival at Mullingar, Stephen descends to the platform with his 'neat little valise', but his arrival passes unnoticed and there is no author's evidence of any welcoming greetings.

Electric light had been installed at Mullingar Railway Station in June 1900, but for such rural sophistication and progress the haughty undergraduate showed no interest.

Westmeath Guardian, 13 April 1900 (extract from full report)

Improvements at Mullingar Railway Station.
They include a new subway to replace the bridge which originally crossed the line. The entrance to the subway is immediately opposite the ticket office window and is surrounded by an ornamental railing, the hall being greatly improved in appearance by the removal of the barrier and gates which formerly extended across this point. The installation of electric light is being rapidly proceeded with. When these improvements are finally perfected, Mullingar Station (save and except Broadstone) will be the finest on the line and in every way worthy of the important town and centre it serves.

ms. 479]
Having passed through the claws of the ticket-collectors, Stephen is sighted by the watchful driver of the small dark-green trap, who enquires if he is the young gentleman for Mr. Fulham. On being assured that this is so they set off together, and we get our first introduction to the condition of the roads of Mullingar by a description of the jolting trap and the oscillating valise. Like almost everything else in the town the trap, according to Stephen is not very clean, but the driver reassures the anxious passenger with a few words and then enquires if he is from Dublin. Having settled this point they fall silent, and the 'ill-groomed hide' of the pony between the shafts is relieved from the torturing attention of flies by the flicking of the whip. There can be no doubt that the unkempt pony matches the trap and the roads, and affords us an early assessment of Mullingar through the author's eyes.

The remainder of this page carries us up the 'long crooked main street of the town', from the Green Bridge to the Dublin Bridge and beyond. The use of the word 'crooked' in the description of this street is hardly justifiable, as the mile-long stretch conforms only to a very gentle 'S' curve; indeed from one point near the half-way mark, a short walk takes one from a clear view of one bridge to an equally clear view of the other.

More puzzling however is the next reference to the 'large square building that stood in grounds closely walled'.

STEPHEN HERO

ms. 480]
he asked the driver what building it was. The driver told him it was the lunatic asylum and added impressively that there were a great many patients in it. The road wound through heavy pasture lands and in [mea] field after field Stephen saw herds of cattle fattening. Sometimes these cattle were in the charge of a drowsy peasant but oftener they were left to themselves and moved slowly from marsh to dry land and from dry land to marsh as the will took them. The little cottages along the road were covered with overblown roses and in many of the doorways there would stand a woman gazing silently over the flat country. Now and again a peasant plodding along the road would give the driver the time of day and if he judged Stephen worthy of the honour fumble at his hat. Proceeding in this manner along the dusty road the trap gradually drew near Mr. Fulham's house.

It was an old irregular house, barely visible from the road, and surrounded by a fair plantation. It was reached by an untended drive and the ground behind it thick with clumps of faded rhododendrons sloped down to the shore

Cape, 241]
of Lough Owel. The lodge was a whitewashed cottage at the door of which a little child in a chemise sat eating a big crust of bread. The gate was open and the trap turned up the drive. After a circular tour of a few hundred yards the trap reached the door of the old discoloured house.

As the trap drew up to the door a young woman advanced to meet it with a quiet dignified gait. She was dressed completely in black and her dark hair was brushed plainly off her temples. She held out her hand:

— Welcome, she said. My uncle is in the orchard. We heard the noise of the wheels.

Stephen touched her hand slightly and bowed.

— Dan, leave that valise in the hall for the present and you, Mr Daedalus, are to come along with me. I hope you are not fatigued by your journey: it is so tiresome travelling.

— Not in the least.

She led the way along the hall and through a little glass door into a great square orchard, the nearer half of which was still a sunny region. Here, screened by a broad straw hat, Mr Fulham was discovered sitting in a basket-chair. He greeted Stephen very warmly and made the usual polite enquiries. Miss Howard had brought out a little tray containing fruit and milk and the visitor gladly ate and drank for the dust of the roads [was] had invaded his throat. Mr Fulham asked a great many questions about Stephen's studies and tastes while Miss Howard stood beside his chair in silence. At a pause in the interrogation she took up the *ms.* 480]

The identification of this building by the driver as the 'lunatic asylum' raises many problems; the main one being that Stephen, going on the road which passes the lunatic asylum would actually be going away from Mr. Fulham's house which, as we learn later is on the shores of Lough Owel. The explanation may be simple, either that the driver misinformed the passenger or that Joyce has made an error of memory. If, on the other hand, the 'large square building' was the County Home, then the driver of the trap was on the Longford Road and heading directly for his destination, but having traversed the length of the town from the railway station the driver could not easily find himself in this area at all unless he had decided to take the longest way round as the shortest way home.

The description of the countryside is slightly romanticized — slow-moving cattle — drowsy peasants — women standing in rose covered cottages gazing over the flat countryside and plodding peasants on the road. Was it any wonder that in later years the Westmeath County Council erected signposts at all the approaches of the town which read 'Mullingar Go Slow'.

Cape, 241] Neither the house which was Joyce's destination nor its occupants can be definitely identified today. From the description given, the particulars of the gate lodge, the winding avenue and the walled orchard, and the mention of Lough Owel, it is possible that the 'old discoloured house' was Levington Park. This house was built in the mid-eighteenth century, and has recently been extensively renovated.

It is a long straggling Georgian residence with an unusual porch set on stout pillars. The most pleasant feature of Levington is its situation overlooking Lough Owel, with its expansive front lawn sweeping gently down almost to the lake shore.

In the year 1900 Levington Park was occupied by W. C. Levinge who was then Secretary of the Westmeath County Council. Since John Stanislaus Joyce would have been working in conjunction with the officers of the County Council, particularly the Secretary, it is possible that some of the work on the electoral list may have been done in Levington Park.

Because of numerous mentions of the 'Bannons', particularly in *Ulysses*, it is possible that one of the Bannon homes, all situated on the western shore of Lough Owel, may have offered a homely hospitality to the Joyce family. None of these houses fit the description given by Joyce in *Stephen Hero*, and there is no memory of the visitors in the area. It should also be mentioned that A. E. Bannon was at this time an official of high standing in the County Council, and had been one of the Councillors who had attempted to 'Raise the Green Flag'.

The poorly clad child with the big crust of bread, sitting at the door of the whitewashed lodge is yet another image of poverty as we enter the grounds of Mr. Fulham's house. The appearance of Miss Howard immediately changes the general picture of decay, and her dignified gait as she approaches matches her dress and hair style. Her formal yet warm welcome seems to usher the reader and her guest into the different world which exists inside her uncle's home. We learn that the trap driver's name is Dan and as he deposits Stephen's valise in the hall, the visitor and Miss Howard go through the house to the orchard where Mr. Fulham is sitting in a basket-chair. Sunshine, warm greetings and polite enquiries greet Stephen's entry, followed by Miss Howard introducing a tray of fruit and milk which are welcome refreshments to the visitor, whose throat has been 'invaded' by the dust of the roads. As the godfather interrogates Stephen on matters of his studies and tastes, Miss Howard stands beside the master's chair in silence.

It is difficult to decide to what degree the names are important, as Stanislaus Joyce recalls in his diary in an entry for 2 February 1904:

> The title (*Stephen Hero*), like the book, is satirical. Between us we rechristened the characters, calling them by names which seemed to suit their tempers or which suggested the part of the country from which they come.
> (Ellmann, *James Joyce*, p. 153)

Again, in an entry in the diary dated 8 September 1907, Stanislaus relates:

> He told me he would omit all the first chapters, and begin with Stephen, whom he will call Daly, going to school, and that he would write the book in five chapters — long chapters.
> The use of the name Dedalus must have seemed for the moment too strange, but it is hard to conceive of Joyce's hero with the name Daly. (Ellmann, *James Joyce*, p. 274)

The relationship between father, son and godfather is expressed earlier. (*Stephen Hero*, pp. 53, 221.) Stephen was threatened by his father that if he did not 'succeed brilliantly' at the coming examination, his university career would come to a close. When the result became known, it was not up to the expectations of Mr. Daedalus, and he 'ransacked his vocabulary in search of abusive terms'. When asked for his plans for the future, the student answered that he had no plans. This led to an ultimatum from father to son:

> Well, the sooner you clear out the better. You've been having us, I see. However, with the help of God and his Holy Mother I'll write to Mullingar the first thing in the morning. There's no use in your godfather wasting any more of his money on you.
> (*Stephen Hero*, p. 221)

Joyce's Mr. Fulham is a fiction, but a daring invention of the author because he is part invention, part real. In the neighbouring county of Meath, there was a Mr. Fulham, an ex-member of parliament for South Meath, who was returned as an anti-Parnellite but unseated on petition on the grounds of clerical and other undue influences brought to bear to secure his return. As we learn later, this man fits the bill as the mythical sponsor of Stephen, but Mr. Fulham is not his godfather; James Joyce's godfather was Philip McCann who had died two years previously and had no relation with Mullingar. Philip McCann appears in *Stephen Hero* and *A Portrait of the Artist* as a student. Whatever the facts, Stephen is more involved with his antagonism toward Miss Howard than other matters, probably in keeping with the wish expressed in a pencil note on page 205 of *Stephen Hero*: 'Stephen wished to avenge himself on Irish women who, he says, are the cause of all the moral suicide in the island.'

STEPHEN HERO

Cape, 242]
tray and carried it into the house. When she came back she offered to show Stephen the orchard and, Mr Fulham returning at the same moment to his newspaper, she led the way down a walk of currant-bushes. Stephen had found his godfather's questions a somewhat severe ordeal and he revenged himself on Miss Howard by a counter-fire of questions concerning the names and seasons and prospects of her plants. She answered all his questions carefully but with the same air of indifferent exactness which marked all her acts. Her presence did not awe him as it had done when he had last met her and he thought that perhaps the uncontaminated nature which he had then imagined accusing him was no more than an unusual dignity of manner. He did not find this dignity of hers very congenial and his new fervour of youth was vitally piqued by her lack of animation. He decided in favour of some definite purpose of hers and against [the] a mechanical discharge of duties and said to himself that it would be an intellectual game for him to discover it. He set this task to himself all the more readily since he suspected that this purpose guiding her conduct must be inimical to his present genial impulses and would probably elude him out of instantaneous distrust and seek natural safety in flight. This fugitive impulse would be prey for him and at once he summoned all his faculties to the chase.

Dinner was served at half past six in a long plainly-furnished room. The table spread under a tall lamp of elegant silver-work wore an air of chaste elegance. It was a slight trial on Stephen's hunger to accept these cold manners and in the warmth of his relish for food he condemned this strange attitude of human beings as ungrateful and unnatural. The conversation was also a little mincing and Stephen heard the words 'charming' and 'nice' and 'pretty' too often to find them agreeable. He discovered the weak point in Mr Fulham's armour very soon; Mr Fulham, like most of his countrymen, was a persuaded politician. Most of Mr Fulham's neighbours were primitive types and he,

Cape, 242] Miss Howard having deposited the tray, and Mr. Fulham having returned to his paper, a convenient interlude arises for the visitor to be taken on a tour of the 'great square orchard'. It is noticeable that this house and orchard possess an interior dimension and impressiveness which greatly transcend their original outside appearance as earlier described by Stephen. The visitor annoyed by his godfather's interrogation, submits the dignified Miss Howard to a similar ordeal regarding the numerous plants, but her air of indifference is unruffled by the counter-fire. The next reference concerning the hostess raises an interesting and very important point concerning the Joyce family connection with Mullingar.

Stephen's statement that Miss Howard's 'presence did not awe him as it had done when he had last met her . . .' (*Stephen Hero*, p. 242); his wondering 'was it raining in Westmeath, (were the cattle standing together patiently in the shelter of the hedges)', (*Stephen Hero*, p. 78); and with his 'mind scampering from Clonliffe College to Mullingar' (*Stephen Hero*, pp. 102-103); all seem to suggest that there had been earlier visits to Mullingar before the 1900-1901 visits. Many other suggestions of a similar nature in other works of James Joyce will be dealt with later in this work.

Miss Howard's 'uncontaminated nature', her dignity and lack of animation annoy Stephen, and he decides on an intellectual strategy to discover the purpose of her demeanour. The 'craftsmanship' of the tall table lamp he admires, but the affectation of the conversation further annoys him and interferes with the enjoyment of his food. The formality and elegance of the 'dinner served at half past six', stress the sense of high social standing and dignity of the household. The 'silver elegance' of the lamp is symbolic of the rare esteem in which his hosts are held, and probably describes the awesome Miss Howard in particular. But the young visitor is impatient to assert himself, and soon the opportunity presents itself when he discovers that Mr. Fulham is a persuaded politician of narrow ideas, living among primitive neighbours who regard him as a man of ripe culture.

If the 'names' in *Stephen Hero* pose problems, so also do 'places'.

> These well-meaning literalists, however, forgot that the writer of a novel — especially a symbolic — impressionist novel — has an obligation to tell a deeper truth than is involved in faithful repetition of the manifest details of the situation. What appear to be distortion and misapplication of "facts", under the skilful hands of the artist, may result in illumination of character.
> (*Time of Apprenticeship — The Fiction of James Joyce*, Marvin Magalaner. Abelard-Schuman, London, 1959.)

No one could argue with the above statement, but 'misapplication or distortion' of topographical detail, even under the skilful hands of the artist, hardly helps to illuminate the local setting of the 'additional pages' of *Stephen Hero*.

When writing *Ulysses*, Joyce was particularly careful about the contemporary Dublin topography of 1904, to the extent, it is said, of using *Thom's Directory* of that year as a constant reference guide when describing the Dublin scene as observed through the eyes of Bloom and Stephen. One of his letters to his Aunt Josephine Murray enquired: 'whether there are trees (and of what kind) behind the Star of the Sea Church in Sandymount visible from the shore and also whether there are steps leading down at the side of it from Leahy's Terrace.' (See Ellmann, *James Joyce*, p. 487.)

The same standards of exact topographical detail were hardly applied in the writing of *Stephen Hero*; indeed there is no reason why one might expect they should, as the work is described as being a 'frankly polemical, expository presentation of his environment'. (*Time of Apprenticeship*. Marvin Magalaner.) But the author himself in a letter to Grant Richards, 5 May 1906, written during the writing of *Dubliners* and the completion of *Stephen Hero* offers a very strong personal opinion on this matter: 'He had written a book,' he informed Grant Richards, 'with the conviction that he is a very bold man who dares to alter in the presentment, still more to deform, whatever he has seen and heard.' (Ellmann, *James Joyce*, p. 218).

Joyce mentions an extraordinary and motley variety of acquaintances: newspaper reporters, railway and ex-railway clerks, money lenders, tea tasters, topers, tipsters, publicans, butchers, doctors, private inquiry agents, clerks in the office of the sub-sheriff, priests, musicians, singers, policemen and prostitutes, to mention but a few. Not forgetting one man who was reputed to have the cure for a dose of the clap! Some of them are named, others, mercifully, remain anonymous, but all very useful people to know for one reason or another.

The identification of Martin Cunningham of *Grace*, in *Dubliners*, with the character of the same name in *Ulysses* and *Finnegans Wake* is well established. M'Coy, Mr. Kernan, Mr. Power and many others who appear in *Dubliners* also make appearances elsewhere in Joyce's works. M'Coy seems to be a distillation of Joyce's own father and Leopold Bloom, and not exactly a blend of the better qualities of either.

Occasionally the reader may come across a character or situation with a vague familiarity; that feeling of 'I have been here before.' 'Leo, the idler', for instance, the 'fat young brother' of *The Encounter*, and 'Nash, the idler', the fat young man of *Stephen Hero* and *A Portrait*, are they the same person? Nash only appears in the 'additional pages' of *Stephen Hero*, but is well represented in *A Portrait* even if only in one scene. (*A Portrait*, pp. 90-93.)

The 'additional' pages of *Stephen Hero* were spared the 'slashing crayon strokes' of the author which appear on other pages. Apart from a few pencil notes on the margins, there are no other signs of re-working the material. Because of this the characters appearing in the 'additional' and the 'five more pages of *Stephen Hero*', may be of special significance, as they may be undisguised.

Cape, 243]
in spite of the narrowness of his ideas, was regarded by them as a man of ripe culture. In a discussion which took place over a game of bézique Stephen heard his godfather explain to a more rustic proprietor the nature of the work done by the missionary fathers in civilising the Chinese people. He sustained the propositions that the Church is also the chief repository of secular culture and that the tradition of learning must derive from the monks. He saw in the pride of the Church the only refuge of men against a threatening democracy and said that Aquinas had anticipated all the discoveries of the modern world. His neighbour was puzzled to discover the whereabouts of the souls of the Chinese people in the other life but Mr Fulham left the problem at the door of God's mercy. At this stage of the discussion Miss Howard, hitherto silent, said that there were three kinds of baptism and her statement was accepted as a closure.

Stephen was a long time in doubt as to the motive of his godfather's patronage. The second day after his arrival as they were driving back from a tennis-tournament Mr Fulham said to him:

— Isn't Mr Tate your English professor, Stephen?

— Yes, sir.

— His people are Westmeath. We often see him during holiday time. He seems to take a great interest in you.

— O, you know him then?

— Yes. He is laid up at present with a bad knee or I'd write to him to come over here. Perhaps we may drive over to see him one of these days . . . He is a very well-read man, Stephen.

— Yes, said Stephen.

Tennis-tournaments, military bands, rustic cricket-matches, little flower shows were [devised] resorted to for Stephen's entertainment. At these functions he remarked that his godfather was very openly humoured and Miss Howard very respectfully courted and he began to suspect that there was money somewhere in the background. These enter-

Cape, 243] The politico-religious discussion which follows is symptomatic of the Midlands, and more particularly the Mullingar malaise of the time. One historian of the 1900's, grinding his own axe, had stated:

> I have no special dislike of Mullingar but it seems to be inhabited by the silliest people in Ireland. The address to Lord Wolseley, which I have before alluded to, read in connection with the speeches made about the Green Flag episode, and, say, a lecture of the late Bishop Nulty's on the water supply of the town, or the correspondence between the present Bishop, Dr. Gaffney, and Lord Greville about the Blessed Virgin, would supply Mark Twain with material for a volume. (M. J. F. McCarthy, B.A., (T.C.D.), Barrister, *Five Years in Ireland,* p. 375. Hodges Figgis, Dublin, 1901.)

Dr. Nulty, Bishop of Meath, 1866 - 1898, had constantly assured the people of Mullingar that he would supply the town and surrounding institutions with what he termed 'his own water', i.e. water pumped from the wells in the grounds of the Loreto Convent. The scheme was abandoned after a bitter and notoriously published squabble which held national and occasionally world headlines for almost twenty years. The Dublin *Evening Mail* report on the matter was quoted in the 21 April 1888 issue of the *Westmeath Examiner* as follows:

> A great war is raging in Mullingar. Dr. Nulty, the Roman Catholic Bishop of Meath, is fighting to death the proprietor of the *Westmeath Examiner,* Mr. John P. Hayden, who is handicapped in the struggle in a most unpleasant way, as he happens to be in jail. Dr. Nulty is a good Nationalist, so is Mr. Hayden, and one would think that the Bishop's charity would prompt him to wait until Mr. Hayden had got out of the Balfourian clutch before opening hostilities.

War was actually declared on Christmas Day, 1886, when Dr. Nulty and Father Callery denounced the newly-elected branch of the National League from the pulpit.

The 'hostilities' inevitably penetrated other fronts, and provided fuel for the pro- and anti-Parnell dispute which was raging.

Only a year earlier, in 1885, Dr. Nulty had been summoned to Rome to explain his extraordinary attitude in favouring the 'nationalisation of land'. On his return, John P. Hayden, as secretary of the Confraternity, read an address of welcome to the bishop, and the whole town turned out to greet their own fearless and victorious advocate of 'the land for the people'.

The bishop's essay on the land question, and his book, *Back to the Land,* published in America in 1887, ranked among the great works of literature. Over a million copes of *Back to the Land* were sold in the U.S.A.

In 1873 Dr. Nulty had recommended Parnell to politics with the following unstinted praise:

> Except for the information contained in a letter which he brought to me from the pastor of the parish in which he lived, I had no knowledge whatever of him. And yet in a single interview of hardly two hours duration, he revealed such extraordinary powers of intellect that I, without the slightest fear of rashness, committed myself to him with the fullest trust and confidence.

By 10 October 1891 the relationship had drastically changed:

> Speaking at first Mass on Sunday last, the Most Rev. Dr. Nulty, referring to the political situation, congratulated the people of Mullingar on being the first to strike a blow at the "pretensions" of Mr. Parnell. They did this by what he called the failure to get a big demonstration for that gentleman when he came to Mullingar some months since, and when he said no merchant in the town would give a plank for the platform, no tradesman drive a nail, no butcher would even provide him with meat to eat.

On 25 March 1893, Dr. Nulty spoke in defence of the Pastoral he had delivered the previous June in Mullingar.

> I believe I must ever regard the North and South Meath Election Petitions as two of the most unpleasant and, perhaps I might add, two of the most painful incidents in my whole life. Parnellism was, avowedly, the cause that created those Election Petitions, and that set in motion the judicial enquiries that followed them. Whether deliberately intended or not, the full force and energy of these two Commissions were directed against my clergy and myself, and aimed at the utter ruin of our reputation and influence; and the temporary success which they achieved was hailed as a larger gain, and a greater victory than the removal of Messrs. Davitt and Fulham from the high and honourable position to which the free votes and voices of their countrymen had fairly raised them.

In 1894 a climax in the 'great war' was reached when Dr. Nulty issued a 'Solemn Edict' which was read in every church in the diocese of Meath. In virtue of his authority as Bishop, and the powers delegated to Bishops by the Holy See, he declared the reading of the *Westmeath Examiner* to be sinful, and that all who should persist in reading it after his condemnation were not fit for the reception of the Sacraments of the Church.

Against this 'edict' Hayden appealed to Rome, but the bishop's action was approved. (*Irish Ecclesiastical Record,* 1894, p. 1141.)

The Examiner office became known as the 'mortal sin' office and Dr. Nulty declared: 'I will not have two pulpits in Mullingar.'

The major parties concerned in the struggle were not above the use of petty sniping and innuendo, and used the public press to vent their spite.

10 August 1895
INFORMATION WANTED
To the Editor, *Westmeath Examiner*

Dear Sir,
You would greatly oblige a number of people in Mullingar if you explain in your next issue what is a "bonnet subscription', about which there has been much talk through the town during the week.

A Catholic (signed)

Editor

We are sorry we cannot afford the information wanted by our esteemed correspondent. An application to the reverend editor of our contemporary might be more successful as rumour says he has some experience in the matter of "bonnet subscriptions", whatever they are.

Ed. W.E.

The 'bonnet subscription' may have had some connection with the P.P. and the collection of girls' hats mentioned by Joyce.

On the broader front of local administration, Mullingar was also making the news. On 14 September 1895, the Mullingar Town Commissioners visited the military barracks to read an address to Lord Wolseley, the new C.i. Chief of the armed forces:

Portions of the address brought under Lord Wolseley's notice were the advantages possessed by Mullingar as a great military centre, owing to the limestone belt on which it is said to be situated (where there is no interference by the bog belt of the district) and the "bone and sinew" making properties it possesses.

In reply, his Lordship laid his finger immediately upon one great requisite of the necessary details for a military station which is wanted in Mullingar, and to which the address made no reference. viz. a water supply. That which exists in Mullingar he describes as very bad, and declared that as long as it continued so, there could be no hope held out that the number of military would be increased. The deputationists took their departure, sadly but quickly. (*Westmeath Examiner*)

This snub to the 'nationalist' Town Commissioners was given wide publicity, and found its way into the history books. Undaunted by the bad press which the Commissioners had received, another local body took the plunge.

The Mullingar Rural District Council were unanimously in favour of the new Irish Movement and made their feelings public. That we as a National District Council beg to congratulate our adopted County man, Mr. John P. Hayden, M.P., for the important work we must have been doing for the Nationalist cause and the United Irish League, when the Castle has thought him a fit subject to be prosecuted, as it shows the importance attached to his utterance, and we pride ourselves out of having such a man in our midst.

In 1897 John P. Hayden was elected M.P. for South Roscommon, filling the vacancy created by the death of his brother. In 1898 in the House of Commons, he proposed an amendment to the Local Government Act of that year. Hayden's amendment, which was carried, proposed that clergymen be disqualified from being members of all elected bodies. There was bitter clerical reaction to Hayden's amendment, and lay members of various Boards accused him of being 'the priest-hunting editor of the *Examiner*'.

The waterworks saga was played out to the last drop, and the curtain was brought down in a dramatic manner. Two notices which appeared in the public press and in *The Westmeath Examiner* are fitting epilogues.

22 December 1900
Windmill at Loreto Convent blown down

The fierce gale which blew over the country on Thursday and extended far into the night did considerable damage to property. In Mullingar, slates were blown off some of the houses and in the outlying country trees were uprooted and other damage of a more or less serious nature was done. The windmill on the grounds of the Loreto Convent, Mullingar, which was used in connection with the pumping of water, succumbed to the fury of the gale, being hurled from the concrete base on which it stood into a quarry adjoining, where it was smashed.

9 November 1901

After many years and numerous difficulties the waterworks of Mullingar may be said to be complete. It is about a quarter of a century since the people of the town started to clamour for a supply of good water. The town is in the centre of an attractive and extensive lake district, and there did not seem to the inhabitants any great or insuperable difficulty to be encountered. Yet obstacle after obstacle arose.

The whereabouts of Limbo, the state of Purgatory, and the future destination of Pagans, particularly the millions of Chinese were favourite subjects of topical speculation in the late nineteenth century. Mr. Fulham's favourable comments on the work being done by the missionary fathers, and his theories regarding the debt of the world to monastic culture were being opposed at that time because of adverse reports from the missionary fields concerning the exploitation of the native people. The suggestion that millions of unbaptized souls were doomed in the afterlife was as open to question as the expected statement from King Edward when taking his oath 'that some twelve millions of his Catholic subjects are idolators'.

The question of idolatry had already been the subject of a series of correspondence between Lord Greville and Bishop Gaffney of Meath, because of a remark made by Lord Greville in the House of Commons concerning the Catholic worship of statues and certain forms of ritualism. Mullingar unanimously condemned the allegations, and called on Lord Greville to resign from the public bodies to which he had been elected by the townspeople. The matter was harmoniously resolved, but not forgotten.

Mr. Fulham wisely relies on the mercy of God to resolve these matters: Miss Howard on the three kinds of Baptism.

Fortunately or otherwise, Mark Twain did not avail of the 'Mullingar Malaise' as material for a volume, but it is safe to say that James Joyce's Parnell themes were deeply influenced by his own first-hand experience of the events in Mullingar at that time.

Stephen is reminded by his uncle that Mr. Tate, his English professor, is also a Westmeath man and a neighbour. Mr. Tate reappears briefly in *A Portrait of the Artist* in a very dramatic fashion when he points his finger at Stephen and accuses: 'This man has heresy in his essay.'

Mullingar in those days was a paradise for a young and impecunious subaltern: of hunting and rough shooting there was no end. The Master of the Westmeath Hounds was Lord Greville, who lived at Clonhugh, and from him and his wife and daughters (one of whom, Veronique, had been at school at Dusseldorf with my sister), Smyths of Gaybrook, Tottenhams of Tudenham, Levinges of Knockdrin, and many others, the hospitality we received was unbounded. (Extract from *Life of an Irish Soldier*, Gen. Sir Alexander Godley.)

The band of the Queen's Own Cameron Highlanders, 3rd Battalion, attended at the opening of the Westmeath Lawn Tennis Club at Ballinderry, Mullingar, on 19 May 1900. The band discoursed a choice programme of music on a day of bright sunshine. During their stay in Mullingar the Camerons were rated as the best behaved regiment ever to visit the town. Joyce, although not mentioning the Camerons in *Stephen Hero*, has some uncomplimentary remarks to make on their behaviour in the Phoenix Park in *Ulysses*, p. 714.

STEPHEN HERO

Cape, 244]
tainments did not amuse the youth; his manner was so quiet that often he passed unnoticed and remained unintroduced. Sometimes an officer would send a glance of impolite inquiry at the cheap-looking white shoes he wore but Stephen always looked his enemy in the face. After a short trial of eyes the youth could usually procure a truce. He was surprised to find that Miss Howard discharged her social duties with such apparent goodwill. He was displeased and disappointed to hear her make a pun one day — a pun which though it was not very clever [but caused] raised a polite laugh from two scrupulous lieutenants. Mr Fulham was old and honoured enough to allow himself the luxury of admonishing publicly whenever occasion arose. [When] One day an officer told a humorous story which was intended to poke fun at countrified ideas [Mr Fulham said:

— Our peasants may be ignorant of many things]

The story was this. The officer and a friend found themselves one evening surprised by a heavy shower far out on the Killucan road and forced to take refuge in a peasant's cabin. An old man was seated at the side of the fire smoking a dirty cutty-pipe which he held upside down in the corner of his mouth. The old peasant invited his visitors to come near the fire as the evening was chilly and said he could not stand up to welcome them decently as he had the rheumatics. The officer's friend who was a learned young lady observed a figure scrawled in chalk over the fireplace and asked what it was. The peasant said:

— Me grandson Johnny done that the time the circus was in the town. He seen the pictures on the walls and began pesterin' his mother for fourpence to see th' elephants. But sure when he got in an' all divil elephant was in it. But it was him drew that there.

The young lady laughed and the old man blinked his red eyes at the fire and went on smoking evenly and talking to himself:

— I've heerd tell them elephants is most natural things,

Cape, 244] Stephen is annoyed at what he considers the excessive interest shown in others while he himself remains unintroduced. He is even more aware of the glances of 'impolite enquiry' at the cheap-looking white shoes he wore. These same white shoes were to remain an eccentric but essential part of Joyce for many years.

There is a similarity between this scene and another recorded in *My Brother's Keeper*, pp. 150-157. (Ellmann, *James Joyce*, p. 155.)

> Two other lyrics that date from about this time were written after an excursion with Mary Sheehy, Francis Skeffington and others into the Dublin hills. Joyce, swaggering a little in his yachting cap and canvas shoes and sporting an ashplant, spent most of his time watching Mary. He admired her beauty, and interpreted her silence in company as a contempt like his for the people around her.

In *A Portrait of the Artist as a Young Man*, the character McCann is Francis Sheehy Skeffington, who died in 1916. (Ellmann, *James Joyce*, p. 63.)

Mullingar Races at Newbrook Race Course drew crowds from all over the country. The course had its own railway siding, and excursions were arranged from Cavan, Sligo, Galway, Castlereagh, Dublin and many other centres. The June meeting was perhaps the most popular, and like Royal Ascot, was something of a fashion parade for the latest in hats and voluminous dresses of the day. The Mullingar Town Plate of 40 Sovereigns and the Clonhugh Plate of the same amount were the principal races, and attracted fields of fifteen to twenty horses.

The introduction of a circus story by Joyce is significant, as Mullingar, with its spacious fair green had always attracted the travelling circus. The 'one night and one night only' tradition was occasionally broken when the 'big top' remained for two or even three nights. Naturally a wealth of story, fact and fiction, was built around the circus, and Mullingar has handed down its own special contributions for posterity.

A group of Mullingar men returning from some business in Dublin decided to avail of the 'bona fide' licensing loop-hole, and stopped off at Kinnegad for a final session before heading for home. Predictably, the drinking continued into the small hours; far beyond the generous allowance made for thirsty travellers. Disaster struck when, without warning, the local Sergeant of Police appeared amongst them. They knew him of course; he had been stationed in Mullingar previous to his transfer to Kinnegad on promotion, and had been 'one of themselves', but now as he produced his notebook, he was a stranger in their midst.

Apart from the Mullingar revellers, there was one other customer in the bar, a Negro lion-tamer from the circus pitched in the field at the back of the school. As might be expected, this man was endowed with a more than usual awareness, and he noticed that, although the Sergeant was making a great show of going through the motions, there was nothing being written in the notebook; nothing in the shape of a Mullingar name or address. Inevitably the lion-tamer's turn came, and his unflinching eyes met the Sergeant's; eyes that had cowed many a big cat in tighter corners than this. As the Sergeant stood with his pencil ready the answer came: 'Me Mullingar man too.'

Like Joyce's 'beef to the heel, Mullingar heifers', Mullingar men also held a special identity! But as Leopold Bloom reminds us when confronting Signor Maffei, the lion-tamer in *Ulysses*: 'All tales of circus life are highly demoralising.' (*Ulysses*, p. 433.)

STEPHEN HERO

Cape, 245]

that they has the notions of a Christian . . . I wanse seen meself a picture of niggers riding on wan of 'em — aye and beating blazes out of 'im with a stick. Begorra ye'd have more trouble with the childre[1] is in it now that[2] with one of thim big fellows.

The young lady who was much amused began to tell the peasant about the animals of prehistoric times. The old man heard her out in silence and then said slowly:

— Aw, there must be terrible quare craythurs at the latther ind of the world.[3]

Stephen thought that the officer told this story very well and he joined in the laugh that followed it. But Mr Fulham was not of his opinion and spoke out against the moral of the story rather sententiously.

— It is easy to laugh at the peasant. He is ignorant of many things which the world thinks important. But we mustn't forget at the same time, Captain Starkie, that the peasant [is] stands perhaps nearer to the true ideal of a Christian life than many of us who condemn him.

— I do not condemn him, answered Captain Starkie, but I am amused.

— Our Irish peasantry, continued Mr Fulham with conviction, is the backbone of the nation.

Backbone or not, it was in the constant observance of the peasantry that Stephen chiefly delighted. Physically,

ms. 490]

they were almost Mongolian types, tall, angular and oblique-eyed. Stephen whenever he walked behind a peasant always looked first for the prominent cheek-bones that seemed to cut the air and the peasants in their turn must have recognised metropolitan features for they stared very hard at the youth as if he were some rare animal[s]. One day Dan was sent into the town to buy some medicine at the druggist's and Stephen went in with him. The trap stopped in the main street before the druggist's and Dan handed down the order to a ragged boy telling him to take it into the shop. The ragged boy first showed the paper to an equally ragged friend and then went into the shop. When they came out they stood at the door of the shop gazing alternately from Stephen to the horse's tail and back again. While they were thus gazing they were confronted by a lame beggar who advanced towards them gripping his stick:

— It was yous called out names after me yesterday.

The two children huddling in the doorway, gazed at him and answered:

— No, sir.

— O yes it was, though.

The beggar thrust his malign face down at their faces and began moving his stick up and down.

— But mind what I'm tellin' you. D'ye see that stick?

---
[1] Children.
[2] 'than' is written in pencil in the margin.
[3] This phrase appears, with changes, in the diary entry for 14 April at the end of the final chapter of *A Portrait of the Artist as a Young Man*.

Cape, 245] Then follows a comment from the old man in an idiom rich as Synge's or Lady Gregory's Kiltartanese. The particular phrase 'the latther ind of the world' was later transferred to *A Portrait of the Artist*, but the idiom is dropped and the phrase appears as 'the latter end of the world'. The old man with the upside-down pipe is transferred from his cabin in Killucan to a cabin in the West of Ireland, and a discussion about the 'universe and the stars' replaces the wonders of the 'elephant with the notions of a Christian' and the other terrible queer creatures at the latter end of the world.

In a letter from James Joyce to his brother Stanislaus, dated 7. 2. '05, the author states:

> Again no old toothless Irishman would say "Divil an elephant"—, he would say "Divil elephant". (Ellmann, *James Joyce*, p. 198.)
> Respectfully I suggest that the old Killucan grandfather would say "Divil d'elephant".

A circus misunderstanding of a different and more sinister nature had caused great alarm in Mullingar a short time previously. Keely and Patterson's Circus was, according to rumour, selected as a target for demolition by the Royal Irish Rifles, the regiment then stationed in town. It was whispered that the soldiers were bent on saturating the tent with paraffin, and setting it on fire during the night performance when the circus would be crowded. In preparation for the proposed assault the people of the town armed themselves, and the traders of Mullingar were completely sold out to the civilians of such defensive weapons as spades, shovels, forks, whips, loading butts and cutlery, not to mention the more easily available pockets of stones and ashplants.

Nothing happened at the night performance, not a single incident, and not for the first time the public had the uneasy feeling that they were had — maybe this time by the shopkeepers!

Mr. Fulham's indignation is hard to fathom, and one cannot blame Stephen for joining in the laugh which followed the elephant story. But Mr. Fulham explains his stand, and ends by reminding his audience that the peasant is perhaps nearer to the true ideal of a Christian life than many of those who condemn him. He also expresses his conviction that the Irish peasantry is 'the backbone of the nation'.

Although these praises of Irish peasantry were being constantly aired by a section of Irish society at the time, this same society took care to keep the peasant in his cabin, with his foot on the bottom rung of the social ladder. The disenfranchised people seemed doomed to a low level of living from which they fought in vain to extricate themselves. The 'backbone of the nation', the true Christian peasantry, was firmly nailed to the rack. Stephen admits his delight in the constant observance of the peasantry as he reservedly qualifies, 'backbone or not'. His physical ethnographical observations which state that the peasants were 'almost mongolian types, tall, angular, and oblique eyed' may raise some eyebrows, even those with epicanthic folds. The author, armed with his medical training, even if very basic, would be aware of the importance of the extensive ethnographical survey which had then been in progress in various parts of the country, particularly on the off-shore islands of the west coast. Professor A. C. Haddon, M.A., and Dr. C. R. Browne were appointed by the Royal Irish Academy for this work, and the result of their joint investigations is published in the *Proceedings of the Royal Irish Academy*, 3rd Series, Vol. VII, 1893, pp. 768-830, pes. XXII-XXIV. Before dismissing Joyce's 'Mongolian types with the oblique eyes' completely, it should be remembered that over a span of even half a century this type of investigation has shown enormous physical changes in progress. In 1893 the men of the Aran Islands were described as being mostly of a slight athletic build, the average height being about 5 feet $4\frac{3}{4}$ inches, whereas that of the average Irishman was then 5 feet $8\frac{1}{2}$ inches. (Haddon and Browne, 1893.) Less than fifty years later the published investigation of Hooton and Dupertius (carried out in 1934-36 and published in 1955) stated that the Aran islanders were taller, with larger and lower heads than any other Irish people, and differed in a number of other measurable characteristics.

The particular physical 'mongolish' traits mentioned by Joyce in describing the Midland peasantry are not as apparent today, but then it is seventy years since the writing of *Stephen Hero*. His own classification of 'metropolitan features' which he says may have distinguished him as some 'rare animal' is hardly a scientific observation, and probably is a device by which Joyce hoped to contrast the sophisticated young Dubliner with the Midland peasantry whom he regards as primitives.

Synge recorded his awareness of the scientific re-awakening through the merry observant eyes of two small farmers, Jimmy and Philly in Act III of *The Playboy of the Western World*. Jimmy boasts of the skulls in the city of Dublin, 'ranged out like blue jugs in a cabin of Connaught'. Philly goes one better and relates: 'It was no lie, maybe, for when I was a young lad there was a graveyard beyond the house with the remnants of a man who had thighs as long as your arm. He was a horrid man, I'm telling you, and there was many a fine Sunday I'd put him together for fun, and he with shiny bones, you wouldn't meet the like of these days in the cities of the world.'

The incident recorded outside the druggist's shop in the town exposes a scene of threatened violence and malevolence, which Stephen was to remember. The episode is reminiscent of the 14 April diary incident of *A Portrait of the Artist* because of Stephen's 'fine chord of terror' at the recollection. The old man with the 'redrimmed horny eyes' of *A Portrait* strikes a similar terror in the author's mind.

> It is with him I must struggle all through this night till day come, till he or I lie dead, gripping him by the sinewy throat till . . . Till what? Till he yield to me? No. I mean him no harm.

The resemblance of the three separate incidents, following each other in *Stephen Hero* and merged in *A Portrait*, is unmistakeable, but may be coincidental.

In *Ulysses*, p. 602, the 'grizzled old veteran irately interrogated: Who's the best troops in the army? And the best jumpers and racers? And the best admirals and generals we've got? . . . The Irish Catholic peasant. He's the backbone of our empire. . . .'

STEPHEN HERO

Cape, 246]
— Yes, sir.

— Well, if ye call out after me the next time I'll cut [yous] yez open with that stick. I'll cut the livers out of ye.

He proceeded to explain himself to the frightened children.

— D'ye hear me now? I'll cut yez open with that stick. I'll cut the livers and the lights out of ye.

This incident was stolidly admired by a few bystanders who made way for the beggar as he limped along the footpath. Dan, who had watched the scene from the trap, now descended to the ground and asking Stephen to look to the horse went into a very dirty public-house. Stephen sat alone in the car thinking of the beggar's face. He had never before seen such evil expressed in a face. He had sometimes watched the faces of prefects as they 'pandied' boys with a broad leather bat but those faces had seemed to him less malicious than stupid, dutifully inflamed faces. The recollection of the beggar's sharp eyes struck a fine chord of terror in the youth and he set himself to whistle away the keen throb of it.

After a few minutes a fat young man with a very red head came out of the druggist's shop holding two neat parcels. Stephen recognized Nash and Nash testified that he recognized Stephen by changing complexion very painfully. Stephen could have enjoyed his old enemy's discomfiture had he chosen but disdaining to do so he held out his hand instead. Nash was junior assistant in the shop and when he learned that Stephen was on a visit to Mr Fulham his manner was tinged with discreet respectfulness. Stephen, however, soon put him at his ease and when Dan emerged from the grimy public-house the two were engaged in familiar chat. Nash said Mullingar was the last place God made, a God-forgotten hole, and asked Stephen how he could stick it.

— I only wish I was back again in Dublin, that's all I know.

— How do you amuse yourself here? asked Stephen.

— Amuse yourself! You can't. There's nothing here.

Cape, 246] The incident of the lame beggar is recorded in one of Joyce's epiphanies, No. xx, published by the Lockwood Memorial Library of Boston in 1956.

> *In Mullingar — an evening in Autumn.*
> THE LAME BEGGAR (*gripping his stick*) . . . It was you called out after me yesterday.
> THE TWO CHILDREN (*gazing at him*) . . . No, Sir.
> THE LAME BEGGAR O, yes it was, though . . . (*moving his stick up and down*) . . . But mind what I'm telling you . . . D'ye see that stick?
> THE TWO CHILDREN Yes, Sir.
> THE LAME BEGGAR Well, if ye call out after me any more I'll cut ye open with that stick. I'll cut the livers out o'ye . . . (*explains himself*) . . . D'ye hear me? I'll cut ye open. I'll cut the livers and lights out o'ye. . . .

The watchful Dan observes the scene from the trap, then handing the charge of the horse over to Stephen, he enters a very dirty-looking public house. This is perhaps an appropriate time to take a peep at the streets of Mullingar and at the traffic.

Traffic on the streets of Mullingar in the early 1900's was undergoing the great changeover which was taking place everywhere. The arrival of the bicycle was greeted with a sort of reluctant enthusiasm, particularly by the conservatives, cleric and lay who considered the new invention rather daring. The horse and the pony and trap were still very much in favour, but at the turn of the century the subject of the bicycle versus the horse was on the agenda for discussion by a meeting of Bishops at Maynooth. The agenda was altered, however, when Dr. William Walsh, Archbishop of Dublin, arrived at the meeting on a bicycle!

Joyce in his own way immortalised the strong-minded bishop in 'Gas From A Burner':

> 'Tis Irish brains that save from doom
> The leaky barge of the Bishop of Rome
> For everyone knows the Pope can't belch
> Without the consent of Billy Walsh.

Despite the example of the trend-setting bishop, the priests in the rural areas held on to the faithful horse who served them, not alone on their parochial rounds, but also at the meets of the Westmeath Hounds and Harriers during the hunting season.

Within a few years County Westmeath could boast of no less than thirteen motor cars, and motor cycles. LI 1, the first registered motor vehicle in Mullingar belonged to a Mr. James from Knockdrin Castle.

An interesting report concerning the motor cars of Westmeath appears in the *Irish Motor News* of 1900-01, Vols. 1 & 2.

> Gather ye knowledge while ye may
> Old fashioned sports are lying dying.
> And those who drive their motors to-day,
> To-morrow may be trying flying.

At the Royal Dublin Society Show at Ballsbrige, 10 - 12 April, Mr. Mecredy, driving Dr. Glenn's Daimler car, led the way on to the track. Mr. James of Knockdrin Castle came next on a splendidly finished eight horsepower four cylindered Panhard which had the record of being the most costly vehicle in the parade.

Joyce was interested in motor cars and roads, and an interview he had with Henri Fournier in Paris, a contender for the Gordon Bennett Cup, is reported in *The Irish Times* of 7 April 1903.

> JOYCE (*Speaking of the speed*) Let me see — then your top speed is nearly eighty-six miles an hour, and your average speed is 61 m.p.h.
> FOURNIER I suppose so if we calculate properly.
> JOYCE It is an appalling pace. It is enough to burn our roads. I suppose you have seen the roads you have to travel. . . .

Westmeath County Council was concerned when some round-the-country rally drivers complained of the poor roads, and replied:

> The roads in County Westmeath are amongst the best in Ireland, and if others were as good as those which the touring party sampled, there would be little reason for complaint.

The condition of the streets of the town of Mullingar gave reason for complaint: in winter-time rain flooded the many potholes, in summer the loose dusty surface blew like a sandstorm.

24 June 1899 — Mullingar watering cart

> Lately they had a dust blowing about, you could observe a blinding dust in the town of Mullingar. If you opened your bedroom window the room and yourself would be covered with dust. Leaving out business altogether, those in private houses have a serious grievance. I have been speaking to many people about the matter and they are in accord with getting the watering cart, and every person to whom I have been speaking seems to think it is a disgrace that such a want has been allowed for so many years past — (another member asked) — Why, until we get the waterworks?

Small wonder the dust of the roads had invaded Stephen's throat as earlier stated on his arrival at Mr. Fulham's home.

Passenger travel on the Royal Canal had long ceased by 1900, but the Royal Canal Company still catered for extensive goods traffic. Photographs taken at the turn of the century show the 'Harbour' at Mullingar piled with merchandise. Joyce, writing to Stanislaus on 25 September 1906, quoted a statement made by Arthur Griffith:

> It costs a Danish merchant less to send butter to Christiania and then by sea to London, than it costs an Irish merchant to send his from Mullingar to Dublin. (Ellmann, *James Joyce*, p. 246)

The population of the town increased steadily during the latter years of the nineteenth century, and at the 1891 census it was recorded as 5,323. This increase was maintained until the middle 1890's, but then the numbers dropped dramatically. The loss of more than ten per cent of the town's population is unexplained, but the resulting havoc is well recorded, and would have exceeded even the most hilarious imaginations of the aforementioned Mark Twain:

25 May 1901. Tit Bits, Westmeath Examiner.

> As the population of the town has fallen below the standard of 5,000 inhabitants, the public houses of the town will in future have to be closed at 10 p.m. Few, even amongst the publicans themselves, will grumble at the change, and whilst it is regrettable and deplorable that the population of the town is going down, it is a matter of congratulations in the interests of humanity and morality that the liquor traffic is curtailed by even one hour every night.

A sobering statement!

Nash, the fat young man with the very red head, who emerges from the druggist's shop now claims Stephen's attention. He is a figure of almost comic relief. The confrontation seems to indicate that Nash and Stephen have had a previous meeting which bore painful memories for Nash. It emerges that they were old enemies, but Stephen manfully offers him the hand of friendship. Could this be the Nash of Mr. Tate's class, who with Heron and Boland had vainly tried to correct Stephen's other literary heresies? (*A Portrait of the Artist*, pp. 90-93.)

STEPHEN HERO

Cape, 247]

— But haven't you concerts sometimes? The first day I came here I saw some bills up about a concert.

— O, that's off. Father Lohan put the boots on that — the P.P.[1] you know.

— Why did he?

— O, you better ask him that. He says his parishioners don't want comic songs and skirt dances. If they want a decent concert, he says, they can get one up in the schoolhouse, — O, he bosses them, I tell you.

— O, is that the way?

— They're afraid of their life[2] of him. If he hears any dancing in a house at night he raps at the window and pouf! out goes the candle.

— By Jove!

— Fact. You know he has a collection of girls' hats.

— Girls' hats!

— Yes. Of an evening when the girls go out walking with the soldiers he goes out too and any girl he catches hold of he snaps off her hat and takes it back with him to the priest's house then if the girl goes to him for it he gives her a proper blowing-up.

— Good man! . . . Well, we must be off now. I suppose I'll see you again.

— Come in tomorrow, will you: it's a short day. And I'll tell you I'll introduce you to a friend of mine here — very decent sort — on the *Examiner*. You'll like him.

— Very good. Until then!

— So long! About two o'clock.

As they drove home together Stephen asked Dan some questions which Dan pretended not to hear and when Stephen pressed him for answers he gave the shortest possible answers. It was plain that he did not care to discuss his spiritual superior and Stephen had to desist.

That evening at dinner Mr Fulham was in genial spirits

---

[1] Parish Priest.
[2] 'lives' is written in pencil in the margin.

Cape, 247] Nash, describing Mullingar as the last place on earth, a godforsaken hole, is only adding to Stephen's own impression which we have already heard, of the very dirty public houses and the peasantry. The town was founded in Anglo-Norman times and few praiseworthy things have been said about it since. In the Elizabethan era the town was of military importance as the numerous State Papers and Calendar Rolls bear witness. In the early 1800's Mullingar had extensive breweries, tan yards, weaving houses for linen and woollen products and a publishing and printing establishment. William Kidd, owner of the printing works, was a publisher of standing in the country and was editor of the *Westmeath Journal,* a weekly newspaper of the late eighteenth and early nineteenth centuries.

An industrial decline in the 1820-30's caused great distress in the town but this situation was partially relieved by the founding of the military barracks, the arrival of the Royal Canal, and eventually the railway.

Writers of those times found Mullingar a dismal place, with more than its share of poverty. William Carleton, who set up a school in the town, described the poverty and distress of the children. Military court martial journals of the time are harrowing documents, recording transportation and death as penalties, often for minor offences.

A phenomenon of the town's population was the number of beggars constantly swarming the streets. In Maxwell's *Wild Sports of the West,* there is a very descriptive chapter of those inglorious mendicants.

By the end of the nineteenth century conditions had improved, but the long delay in installing a waterworks and sewage scheme hindered progress. Dr. J. Dillon Kelly, M.O.H., described the serious insanitary condition of the town's sewers in 1899.

> The foregoing may be taken as a fair description of all the sewers of the town, which by one way or another, run into the main sewer, namely, the Brosna. An idea may be formed of this river which bisects the town, running from North to South, when it is understood that it carries in its waters sewage from the barracks, workhouse, asylum, and infirmary, before it meets that of the town and the jail!

The conversation now switches to amusements or the lack of them.

The cancelled concert which Fr. Lohan, the parish priest, had 'put the boots on', was, according to Nash, an advertised affair of the comic song and skirt dance variety! The entertainments in the school obviously rivalled the activities in the Lecture Room, now St. Mary's Hall, which was then occasionally used as a school room during day classes for the girls. House dancing and crossroad dancing had long been discouraged because of drink abuses, as had been the custom of all-night wakes.

A crossroads piper musician, well known and respected, who defied the ban, fell foul of his parish priest who, in revenge, confiscated the pipes. To the consternation of his curate, the musical P.P. spent most of the nights during the following months teaching himself to drag a wheezy tune from the reluctant pipes. The resulting nocturnal groans and moans made life in the parochial house a near hell for all concerned.

For many years after these events it was still the custom for men to play the female roles in the plays and sketches. Female players were not allowed, as the parish priest of the time and his later followers in office had strong views on the matter of mixed casting!

> 17 November 1900.
> St. Mary's Temperance Society, Mullingar.
> Performance by the dramatic class.
> Scenery: Frank Russell,
> assisted by John Moran as Stage Manager.
>
> A production of the Irish drama, *Arrah-na-Pogue,* or *The Wicklow Wedding,* was given by the Amateur Dramatic Class of the St. Mary's Temperance Society, Mullingar, in the Lecture Hall on Tuesday night. Looked at from every point of view the performance was a splendid success. . . . Not a flaw could be detected in the characterization, and all round there was given a display of histrionic ability which was seldom equalled but never surpassed in local circles. . . . In the role of "Fanny Power", Mr. Joseph Dargan, owing to sex, had a difficult portion to discharge, but he did his part with a freedom, grace, and ability that could not very well be excelled on the amateur stage. . . . The string band of the Cameron Highlanders, by permission of Colonel the Mackintosh of Mackintosh, attended and played some very nice selections.

Could the distinguished Col. the Mackintosh of Mackintosh bear any relationship to the mysterious McIntosh, whose inclusion in the list of mourners at Dignam's funeral in *Ulysses* is described as one of the celebrated riddles in the book?

A concert of the 'Comic songs and skirt dances' was advertised in *The Westmeath Guardian,* 13 April 1888.

> On Monday night next Miss Maggie Morton and her Comedie Anglaise Company will commence a six nights' engagement in the Lecture Hall. Miss Morton, in her several visits to this town, has secured for herself a deservedly high reputation, but independent even of this, the pieces announced for production — "The Unknown" — "Castle" — "Ours" — "As You Like It" — "School" — and "Hazel Kirke" — should warrant crowded houses each night.

A different kind of entertainment was promised for 31 August 1901:

> One of the most interesting events in the near future in Mullingar will undoubtedly be the concert on the 10th inst., at which Mr. Percy French and a number of distinguished local and other vocalists and instrumentalists will take part. Mrs. E. Shaw, Mullingar, will be the violin soloist on the occasion.

Even Fr. Lohan could scarcely resist the plaintive call for Paddy Reilly to return to his native Ballyjamesduff!

The story of the P.P. and the ladies' hats was well known in Mullingar, and had numerous variations. Courting the 'soldiers' was an unforgivable crime and many young girls, and some not so young, were ostracized for years by the townspeople for fraternizing with the garrison.

A version of the 'hat story' tells of a certain clergyman whose intervention misfired. A surprised soldier released his young lady when challenged and apologised profusely to the Reverend intruder for stealing his girlfriend, and on many further meetings with the reverend gentleman insisted on repeating the apology.

With a promise of introduction to a 'very decent sort' from the *Examiner* on the following day, the friends part.

Silent Dan's reluctance to discuss, much less denounce his spiritual superior to the inquisitive Stephen is understandable. Holding forth on 'Clerical Oppression' within the walls of a public house, surrounded by natives was one thing; to express the same sentiments openly to a stranger was out of the question.

Apart from matters of politics, pollution and religion, the town had other more delicate problems.

11 May 1900: *Westmeath Guardian*
Mullingar Town Commissioners.
The usual monthly report of the Town Sergeant having been read, Mr. Murtagh said he never mentioned anything about the morality of the town.

CHAIRMAN	Have you any report?
TOWN SERGEANT	I have not.
MR. MURTAGH	I said that the matter should be reported.
CHAIRMAN	The thing has been a dead letter in Mullingar for years, and it is not right.
MR. MURTAGH	Is that so, sir?
CHAIRMAN	It looks like it.
MR. MURTAGH	I know he is doing his duty in other respects but I would be glad to see him reporting regularly on the morality of the town, because it would have an effect. It should be shown here every month.

STEPHEN HERO

Cape, 248]

and began to address his conversation pointedly to Stephen. Mr Fulham's method of 'drawing' his interlocutor was not a very delicate method but Stephen saw what was expected of him and merely waited till he was directly addressed. A neighbour had come to dinner, a Mr Heffernan. Mr Heffernan was not at all of his host's way of thinking and therefore the evening brought out some lively disputes. Mr Heffernan's son was learning Irish because he believed that the Irish people should speak their own language and not the language of their conquerors.

— But the people of the United States who are more emancipated than Ireland is ever likely to be are content to speak English, said Mr Fulham.

— The Americans are different. They have no language to revive.

— For my part I am content with my conquerors.

— Because you occupy a good position under them. You are not a labourer. You enjoy the fruits of Nationalist agitation.

— Perhaps you are going to tell me that all men are equal, said Mr Fulham satirically.

— In a sense they may be.

— Nonsense, my dear sir. Our countrymen know nothing of the Reformation, as they call it, and I hope [it] they will know nothing of the French Revolution either.

Mr Heffernan returned to the charge.

— But surely it is no harm for them to know something about their country — its traditions, its local history, its language!

— For those who have leisure it may be good! But you know I am a great enemy of disloyal movements. Our lot is thrown in with England.

— The young generation is not of your opinion. My son, Pat, is studying in Clonliffe at present and he tells me all the young students there, those who are to be our priests afterwards, have these ideas.

Cape, 248]

The awareness of national identity and culture as expressed by Mr. Heffernan was ever present, even in the hearts of emigrants, as this letter from London regarding the *Arrah-na-Pogue* performance of the previous week shows:

21 November 1900.
To the Editor, *Westmeath Examiner*.

Why in the name of fair play was the band of the Cameron Highlanders engaged to provide music at what should have been a purely Irish entertainment? It is difficult to hope to have anything native when such a society as St. Mary's engages an army band, while, may be, local bands are dying for want of patronage. But perhaps a workingman's band would not be respectable enough to perform before the convent educated young ladies of Mullingar. I suppose if an army band were not available a German band would have been engaged. Social Ireland is rotten!

J. M. F., London.

Mr. Heffernan points out that his son Pat, studying in Clonliffe, and other students had 'these ideas' — an awareness of the history and traditions of the country, and a knowledge of its language.

Joyce's attitude to the learning and speaking of the Irish language and to the Gaelic League is covered in Chapter XVII of *Stephen Hero*. Following a prolonged argument on subjects of literature, language, peasantry and morality, Stephen lyingly expresses a wish to learn Irish. His only interest in the language class, however, is to make the acquaintance of Emma Clery who is already enrolled as a pupil. Seeing the lie through, he buys the necessary books, but refuses to pay any subscriptions to the Gaelic League, or wear its badge in his buttonhole.

He describes the meetings, and in particular the teacher. This 'young man with spectacles, a very sick looking face and a very crooked mouth', who stressed that English was the language of commerce and Irish the language of the soul was in reality Patrick Pearse, and the language class in the room in O'Connell Street really took place in University College (Ellmann, *James Joyce*, p. 62). Because of the attitude of his teacher it seems that Joyce abandoned the classes.

In 1900 a branch of the Gaelic League had been formed in Mullingar with the patriotic editor of the *Westmeath Examiner* as one of its active sympathizers. The Gaelic or Celtic Revival, as it was then called, aroused no great enthusiasm in the town, and the Gaelic League was faced with the unenviable task of instructing reluctant students. Nevertheless, sentiments such as those expressed by Mr. Heffernan were often voiced, but the activities of the National League and the United Irish League were considered much more important than the minority involvement of the language movement.

Yet, strangely enough, in the following year it was proposed and passed at a meeting of the Mullingar Town Commissioners on 13 July 1901, that name boards in English and Gaelic be erected for the streets. Mullingar would show the way!

STEPHEN HERO

Cape, 249]

— The Catholic Church, my dear sir, will never incite to rebellion. But here is one of the young generation. Let him speak.

— I care nothing for these principles of nationalism, said Stephen. I have enough bodily liberty.

— But do you feel no duty to your mother-country, no love for her? asked Mr Heffernan.

— Honestly, I don't.

— You live then like an animal without reason! exclaimed Mr Heffernan.

— My own mind, answered Stephen, is more interesting to me than the entire country.

— Perhaps you think your mind is more important than Ireland!

— I do, certainly.

— These are strange ideas of your godson's, Mr Fulham. May I ask did the Jesuits teach you them.

— The Jesuits taught me other things, reading and writing.

— And religion also?

— Naturally. 'What doth it profit a man to gain the whole world if he lose his soul?'

— Nothing, of course. That is quite so. But humanity has claims on us. We have a duty to our neighbour. We have received a commandment of charity.

— I hear so, said Stephen, at Christmas. Mr Fulham laughed at this and Mr Heffernan was stung.

— I may not have read as much as you, Mr Fulham, or even as much as you, young man, but I believe that the noblest love a man can

Stephen Hero in Mullingar

Cape, 249] Few would have agreed with Mr. Fulham's statement that 'our lot is thrown in with England', but later when the war loomed some opinion swayed in that direction. Local bodies and County Councils, since the disbandment of the Grand Jury System, were becoming increasingly and more outspokenly 'disloyal' to oppressive authority. At the meeting held in the Market House to condemn the action of the High Sheriff regarding the removal of the green flag, Mr. Goff suggested with fervour that the national flag should be hoisted, not alone over every courthouse, but also over every labourer's cottage and farmhouse in Westmeath. Mr. Fulham displays a sad ignorance of 'his countrymen' when he states that 'they know nothing of the Reformation, and will know nothing of the French Revolution'.

During a speech made at Gorey on 23 August 1885, William Smith O'Brien stated:

> In the better days that are approaching, the soil of Ireland will be populated by a race of Irishmen free and happy and thriving, owing no master under the Almighty, and owing no flag but the *green flag* of an Independent Irish Nation.
> (*United Ireland,* 29 August 1885)

Fourteen years later, in September 1899, following a resolution previously passed, and against the authority of the High Sheriff, Capt. the Hon. R. F. Greville, the members of the Westmeath County Council arrived at the Court House to erect the green flag. After a hurried meeting attended by Lord Greville and Mr. Barnes, the councillors decided to abandon the Court House and hold their meeting on the public street. The people of the town claimed the Court House was their own property and under their control in the person of the constitutionally formed Westmeath County Council. The High Sheriff and others disputed the claim, and threatened to lock the public out. To bring matters to a head the councillors decided to precipitate a crisis by raising the green flag.

Extra police had been summoned for the expected confrontation, and before an estimated crowd of 1,500 people the councillors charged the guard, waving the flag, and attempting to gain admission through the now locked and barred gateway. After a battle royal the councillors were eventually given permission to enter through the main gateway, but as soon as the gateway was opened the crowd charged and a near-riot situation developed. Several times the flag was erected and snatched down, until eventually it was confiscated. Later, the crowd and some of the councillors, battered and bloody, dispersed, and held meetings elsewhere.

Mr. Awley E. Bannon, D.C., was remembered as the man who

> carried the old flag into the enemy's camp, and what was formerly the enemy's citadel, and hung it from the window of what was once the stronghold of ascendancy in that country.

The 'baton charge in the Grand Jury Room' was one of the great occasions recorded in the history of the town, and made headlines for many years as 'The day they raised the Flag in Mullingar'.

Stephen is requested to express his own opinions on these matters and he is very definite and embarrassing to his elders in his views. When he admits that 'my own mind is more important than Ireland', he is restating something he first said to W. B. Yeats in 1902, and was later to repeat in *Ulysses* in a slightly changed form. He never changed his opinion, a fact revealed when Joyce was visited years later by Simone Téry—'the French journalist who admired equally Russian Communism and Irish Mysticism.'

'Do you think Irish self-government a good thing?' she asked him.

'I don't think anything about it,' Joyce replied unhelpfully.

'What is your attitude towards the national movement in Ireland?' she pressed him.

'To use an expression of your own country, *j'en ai marre* (I'm fed up with it).'

'I think you were already fed up with it twenty years ago.'

Joyce nodded. 'You could say forty.'

(Simone Téry, *L'ile des Bardes* (Paris 1925), quoted in Maria Jolas, ed. *A James Joyce Yearbook,* Paris (1949) p. 189. (Ellmann, *James Joyce,* p. 582.)

The pomposity of Stephen annoys Mr. Heffernan, and he challenges the young upstart about the Jesuitical teaching on certain subjects. Stephen admits that the Jesuits taught him reading, writing and religion. 'What doth it profit a man to gain the whole world if he lose his soul?' Heffernan counters by reminding Stephen of the commandment of charity, but the young visitor turns the tables again by admitting that charity is heard of at Christmas! Mr. Fulham laughs at his godson's cynical remark and Mr. Heffernan admits that although he may not have read as much as either of his opponents, 'yet he believed that the noblest love a man can. . . .'

STEPHEN HERO

ms. 498]
have, of course after the love of God, is love of his native land.

— Jesus was not of your opinion, Mr. Heffernan, said Stephen.

— You speak very boldly, young man, said Mr. Heffernan reprovingly.

— I am not afraid to speak openly, answered Stephen, even of the parish priest.

— You use the Holy Name glibly for one so young.

— Not in execration. I mean what I say. The ideal presented to mankind by Jesus is one of self-denial, of purity, and of solitude; the ideal you present to us is one of revenge, of passion and of immersion in worldly affairs.

— It seems to me that Stephen is right, said Miss Howard.

— I can see, said Mr. Fulham, what these movements tend to.

— It is impossible for us all to live the lives of hermits! exclaimed Mr. Heffernan desperately.

— We can combine the two lives by living as a Catholic should, doing

Cape, 249]
our duty to God first and then the duties of our station in life, said Mr Fulham, leaning comfortably on the last phrase.

— You can be a patriot, Mr Heffernan, said Stephen, without accusing those who do not agree with you of irreligion.

ms. 498] Stephen's retort that Jesus, the founder of Christianity, did not think that way shocks Mr. Heffernan, but the glib young visitor goes on and reminds his audience that he is not afraid to speak openly, even of the parish priest! The real ideals of Christianity as opposed to the tainted worldly ideals of Mr. Heffernan are expressed in no uncertain terms, and Stephen finds an ally in a most unexpected quarter when Miss Howard admits that it seems to her that Stephen is right. This calling of Stephen by his Christian name seems to suggest that Miss Howard's indifference has now been replaced by a new awareness of her visitor, with perhaps, a promise of further developments. Mr. Fulham sums up by introducing a compromise: the Catholic way of life which observes both duties; but Stephen has the last word when he reminds Mr. Heffernan that 'you can be a patriot without accusing those who disagree with you of irreligion'. Stephen, who had set out to see how his orthodox audience would stand up to the guns of orthodoxy had succeeded in drawing them into his own arena, even Miss Howard.

Clerical influence and interference in politics had recently been replaced by the much more efficient weapon, clerical participation. 'I'll pay your dues, father, when you cease turning the house of God into a polling booth.' The remark, made by a friend of Mr. Daedalus to the canon as described in the Christmas dinner scene in Chapter I of *A Portrait of the Artist as a Young Man*, had now a new significance.

It would appear to most observers in the town of Mullingar that the pulpit was not alone the polling booth, but the very seat of government. The townspeople had been congratulated from the pulpit on being the first to strike a blow at the 'pretensions' of Mr. Parnell, but they wore the laurel uneasily. It was all very well for Stephen, in the final statement on page 216, to remind Mr. Heffernan that he could be a patriot without accusing those who disagreed with him of irreligion, but was it patriotism or religion one expected from the pulpit? The ammunition with which Stephen has loaded his 'guns of orthodoxy' was, of course, his own particular brand of Jesuitical and Aquinas argument. Mr. Fulham agrees with the principles of Aquinas' teaching regarding the interdependence of the laws of human origin and the laws of nature, but his genial 'we all understand each other' is too hopeful, especially regarding Mr. Heffernan.

Stephen attributes his godfather's patronage, not to Aquinas, but to his respect for feudal distinctions, and submission to the dispenser of these distinctions. The author's own feelings on these matters had undergone a dramatic change over the years. He had earlier expressed his current philosophy to McCann in the porch of the College Library:

> ... All modern political and religious criticism dispenses with presumptive States, [and] presumptive Redeemers and Churches. [and] It examines the entire community in action and reconstructs the spectacle of redemption. If you were an esthetic philosopher you would take note of all my vagaries because here you have the spectacle of the esthetic instinct in action. ...
>
> (*Stephen Hero*, p. 191)

In *A Portrait*, when the Dean asks Stephen as to when they might have something from him on the esthetic question, he answers that he only stumbles on an idea once a fortnight if lucky! The student admits that at present to suit his purpose he is working by the light of one or two ideas of Aristotle and Aquinas.

> — I see. I quite see your point.
> — I need them only for my own use and guidance until I have done something for myself by their light. If the lamp smokes or smells I shall try to trim it. If it does not give light enough I shall sell it and buy another.
>
> (*A Portrait of the Artist*, pp. 212-213)

Cape, 250]
— I never accused . . .
— Come now, said Mr Fulham genially, we all understand each other.

Stephen had enjoyed this little skirmish: it had been a pastime for him to turn the guns of orthodoxy upon the orthodox ranks and see how they would stand the fire. Mr Heffernan seemed to him a typical Irishman of the provinces; assertive and fearful, sentimental and rancourous, idealist in speech and realist in conduct. Mr Fulham was harder to understand. His championing of the Irish peasant was full of zealous patronage, his ardour for the Church was implicit with his respect for feudal distinctions, and his natural submission to what he regarded as the dispenser of these distinctions. He would enforce his aristocratic notions in a homely way:

— Come now, Mr So and So, you buy cattle on fair-day in the town?
— Yes.
— And you go[1] the racecourse and make a bet or two as you fancy?
— I must admit I do.
— And you pride yourself on knowing a thing or two about coursing?
— I think I do.
— Then how can you say there is no aristocracy of breed in men since you know it exists in animals?

Mr Fulham's pride was the pride of the burgher in the costly burdensome canopy which he has exerted[2] and loves to sustain. He had affection for the feudal machinery and desired nothing better than that it should crush him — a common wish of the human adorer whether he cast himself under Juggernaut or pray God with tears of affection to mortify him or swoon under the hand of his mistress. To the sensitive inferior his charity would have offered intolerable pain of mind and yet the giver would use neither the

[1] 'to' omitted.
[2] 'Erected' (?)

Stephen Hero in Mullingar

Cape, 250] The feudal 'hangover' of equating aristocracy of breed in animals with that of humans was a noted feature of the time, and common to all classes. The peasant, himself a good judge of the 'points' of a horse or a beast, often, like his master, applied these terms of reference in assessing his fellow man or woman. Thus, humans were placed in the equine categories of colts and fillies, and the broader bovine qualification of 'Beef to the heels like a Mullingar heifer'.

The peasant loved the hunt but not the huntsman. There was a softening of this attitude later when most farmers kept a hunter and participated in the chase. The clergy might challenge Lord Greville's accusations of 'idolatry' and 'ritualism', but not at a meeting of the Hunt.

There are numerous accounts of peasants frustrating the hunt by interfering with coverts or actually blocking the course. Such interference was almost always resolved amicably, and afforded yet another opportunity for the Lord to extol the excellent qualities of 'his' peasantry, while attempting to anticipate their next move in an effort to forestall it. A well-known story of the era tells of the genuine amazement expressed by the newly-married Lord and Lady at the thought that their coachman, also newly married, might be sharing similar conjugal bliss.

Mr. Fulham would understand the Lord's justifiable uneasiness; Stephen might even enjoy it.

The Most Rev. Dr. Gaffney, Bishop of Meath, in the course of a letter to the Rev. W. P. Kearney, P.P., Kinnegad, Treasurer of the Election Fund, dated 6 October 1900, stated:

> I am no silent advocate of the land for the people, and Mr. Davitt used my pronouncements on the subject as his text in Mullingar with approval and endorsement and many compliments. If Mr. Kennedy were unsound on the land question and I were his sponsor, I would serve to share his fate. It is not the land question, it is not politics, it is party, and unfortunate Ireland is only a secondary question in importance to their personal and party squabbles. The leaders do not want able, sturdy men of Irish blood; they want creatures responsive to their every whim. It would be a woeful day for Ireland if we had only one newspaper, one ruler, or even a triumvirate — and this is the goal that is sought.

At the handing in of the nomination papers, Father O'Reilly, P.P., Mullingar, reminded the people of Mullingar:

> The motto on our banner is Priests and People, faith and fatherland — Mullingar had always been true to its bishops and priests, and to Ireland. Mullingar would hoist the green flag yet!

Dante, or Mrs. Riordan at the Christmas Dinner in *A Portrait of the Artist* was right, no more could politics be divided from religion; it was a question of public morality. 'A priest would not be a priest if he did not tell his flock what is right and what is wrong.' It was heresy to think otherwise.

The counter-accusations and denials of Mr. Heffernan and Mr. Fulham represent the distinctive gulf which existed between the idealist peasant on one hand and the aristocratic feudal lord on the other. They championed and were dependent on each other, but indulged in endless futile justifications of the attitudes and ideals which kept them apart.

Mr. Fulham wishes to be reunited with the natural order which transcends man-made systems. Mr. Heffernan exhibits a characteristic trait of the peasantry: an unusual agility to agree with everything without committing himself to anything.

STEPHEN HERO

Cape, 251]
air nor the language of the self-righteous. His conceptions of human relations [would] might perhaps have passed for a progressive conception in the ages when the earth was thought to be scaphoid and had he lived then he might have been reputed the most [tender-hearted] enlightened of slave-owners. As Stephen watched the old man gravely handing his snuff-box to Mr Heffernan, and the latter perforce appeased, inserting a large hand therein [Stephen] he thought: [to]

— My godfather is the Papal ambassador to Westmeath.

Nash was waiting for him at the door of the shop and they walked down the main street together towards the *Examiner* office. In the window [was] a white fox-terrier's [muzzle] head could be seen over a dirty brown blind and his intelligent eyes were the only signs of life in the office. Mr Garvey was sent for and presently sent in word that his two visitors were to come into the *Greville Arms*. Mr Garvey was found sitting at the bar with his hat pushed far back from a glowing forehead. He was 'chaffing' the barmaid but when his visitors entered he stood up and shook hands with them. Then he insisted on their joining him in a drink. The barmaid was 'chaffed' again by Mr Garvey and by Nash but always within limits. She was a genteel young person of a very tempting figure. While she was polishing glasses she indulged in flirty, gossipy conversation with the young men: she seemed to have the life of the town at her fingers' ends. She reproved Mr Garvey once or twice for levity and asked Stephen wasn't it a shame for a married man. Stephen said it was and began to count the buttons of her blouse. The barmaid said Stephen was a nice sensible young man not a gadabout fellow and smiled very sweetly over her brisk napkin. After a while the young men left the bar, first touching the fingertips of the barmaid and raising their hats.

Mr Garvey whistled the terrier out of the office and they set off for a walk. Mr Garvey wore heavy boots and he plodded along sturdily in them, tapping the road with his

Stephen Hero in Mullingar

Cape, 251] Stephen's assessment of his godfather is interesting: 'A proud feudal baron wishing destruction from the machinery he so carefully maintained.' He relegates Mr. Fulham to the age of slavery when the earth was thought to be scaphoid — and was believed to be a boat sailing through the universe. But the passing of the snuff box to Mr. Heffernan by the godfather opens a new dimension in Stephen's mind — he now decides that Mr. Fulham is the 'Papal ambassador to Westmeath'.

Joyce's 'Papal ambassador' is a puzzling creation and cannot be traced in ecclesiastical records. It may have some connection with an unorthodox army called the Papal Brigade which was organized in the 1880's to go to Rome and fight for the Pope. The incident was much in the news locally, as a man from Walshestown, on the west shore of Lough Owel, had been one of the three from Westmeath who joined. But Mr. Fulham's ardour for the Church would never lead to taking up arms; like his aristocratic notions, he would enforce his zeal in a homely way, but nevertheless enforce it!

Back in the town of Mullingar, Nash and Stephen walk down the main street towards the *Examiner* office. The *Westmeath Examiner* office was then situated in Earl Street, now Pearse Street. The paper was founded in 1882, the year Joyce was born, by John P. Hayden, who was for many years M.P. for South Roscommon. He was a staunch Parnellite and had been jailed on a few occasions for his outspoken nationalism. Mullingar, however, had literally refused to accommodate Hayden with a platform when Parnell visited the town — the publicans would not loan the porter barrels on which to erect the platform timbers. As might be expected, the outspoken Editor ran afoul of the town fathers, cleric and lay. His long feud with Dr. Nulty on the mundane but vital matter of the Mullingar water-works is a classic comedy situation in its own right, with Hayden playing the role of victim.

Passing the *Examiner* office, Stephen observes the head of a white fox terrier. Next the scene moves into the *Greville Arms Hotel* where we are introduced to Mr. Garvey and later the barmaid.

The *Greville Arms Hotel* is a nineteenth-century building and stands adjacent to a group of houses, one of which housed the Bianconi stables and depot. Earlier the site was occupied by a jail, which was also remarkable for its hospitality; at least it was always full.

In the *Egmont Manuscripts* (1905, I - II, pp. 74 - 75) an amusing incident concerning this gaol is recorded.

> 6 May 1597.
> Jane Hopp, widow, keeper of the gaol at Molyngare (Mullingar), Co. Westmeath, to pay a fine of 200 l and to be imprisoned during pleasure, for having allowed two notorious traitors of the sept of the Newgents to escape — although the Justices had given her a special charge to look to them carefully. . . . Whereby great trouble and garboyle is likely to happen in that county. . . .

A prophetic statement; on 8 July 1642, the town was burned to the ground!

In *Pigots Commercial Directory* of 1824, the *Greville Arms* was known as Wilton's Hotel, later named Murray's, and was purchased by Lord Greville in 1858 when he purchased the entire town for £120,000, which afforded his Lordship an annual rental of £6,000. The present heraldic symbol used by the hotel was granted to the first Baron Greville of Cloyne, Co. Westmeath, on 15 December 1869.

In the *Westmeath Examiner* of 10 June 1899, the following notice appeared:

> The announcement in another column that the business of the Greville Arms Hotel, Mullingar, will be carried on in future by Mr. M. J. Carroll, son of the late proprietress, on the lines which in the past made it such a favourite resort, will be read with pleasure by many in the county and by strangers whose business takes them to Mullingar from time to time.
>
> Under its new management the hotel is certain to sustain, if indeed it does not surpass, the high reputation which it has so worthily maintained for many years.

Garvey, the reporter from the *Examiner* office, the 'very decent sort' mentioned earlier by Nash, is discovered in the *Greville Arms Hotel*, sitting at the bar, with his hat pushed back from a glowing forehead. He is a newly-married young man and since coming to work on the *Examiner* has reformed his boozing habits, but he is only partly reformed as we discover by his flirtatious levity with the barmaid. The amusing scene in the hotel bar, depicted with brief but striking detail, needs little comment. The pompous Stephen admits annoyance at the levity of his coarse companion, Garvey; and predictably, as always in past similar encounters, emerges as 'a nice sensible young man, not a gad-about fellow'. They leave after a while, touching the fingers of the barmaid, 'who had the life of the town at her fingers' ends', and raising their hats in farewell.

STEPHEN HERO

Cape, 252]
stick. The road and the actual sultry day had made him sensible and he gave the younger men some sound advice.

— After all, there's nothing like marriage for making a fellow steady. Before I got this sit on the *Examiner* here I used knock about with the lads and boose [a][1] bit . . . You know, he said to Nash — [Na]sh[1] nodded.

— Now I've a good house, said Mr Garvey, and . . . I go home in the evening and if I want a drink . . . well, I can have it. My advice to every young fellow that can afford it is: marry young.

— There's something in that, said Nash, when you've had your fling, that is.

— O, yes, said Mr Garvey. By the bye I hope you'll come and see me some evening and bring your friend. You'll come, Mr Daedalus? The missus'll be glad to see you: she plays a bit, you know.

Stephen mumbled his thanks and decided that he would endure severe bodily pain rather than visit Mr Garvey.

Mr Garvey began then to tell some press stories. When he heard from Nash that Stephen was inclined for writing he said:

— You take my tip: shorthand.

He told many stories illustrating his own smartness at his business and said that he had once got a 'par' into a London morning paper and got paid well for it by return of post.

— These English chaps, you know, they know how to do business. Pay good money too.

The day was very hot and the town seemed dozing in the heat but when the young men came to the canal bridge they noticed a crowd collected some fifty yards off on the canal bank. A butcher's boy was telling a circle of workmen about it.

— I seen her first. I noticed something — a long-looking green thing lying among the weeds and I went for Joe Coghlan. Him and me tried to get it up but it was too heavy. So

[1] Manuscript torn.

Cape, 252] The intelligent dog is whistled out of the office. The party heads east down the town towards the Dublin Bridge. The open air seems to bring some sensible sobriety into the mind of Mr. Garvey, and he proceeds to advise his young listeners on such subjects as marriage and drinking habits. Nash replies drily that there's something in that when you've had your fling. Garvey seems to be aware of Joyce's musical ability, informing him that his wife 'plays a bit' and that she would be glad to see them. This is the last straw as far as Stephen is concerned; he feels he would endure severe bodily pain rather than visit Mr. Garvey or his musical wife. He thanks him, nevertheless, for the kind thought.

This scene is reminiscent of the walk of Bloom and Stephen in the quiet night streets of Dublin which ends with their singing together a version of 'The Low Backed Car'. As they pass the horse-drawn street sweeper, they pause to speculate on the horse and its worth. Then they recall other animals, including the mongrel in Barney Kiernan's tavern, but the recollection is interrupted abruptly by Bloom:

'What's this I was saying? Ah, yes! My wife, he intimated, plunging *in medias res*, would have the greatest pleasure in making your acquaintance, as she is passionately attached to music of any kind.' (*Ulysses*, p. 624.) Both scenes are a preparation for a change of mood; from a happy-go-lucky saunter to a grave encounter.

The description of the walk through the streets which follows is also recorded in one of Joyce's Epiphanies, No. XIX:

(Mullingar. A Sunday in July. noon.)
TOBIN (*walking noisily with thick boots and tapping the road with his stick.*)
O there's nothing like marriage for making a fellow steady. Before I came here to the *Examiner* I used knock about with fellows and boose. . . . Now I've a good house and . . . I go home in the evening and if I want a drink . . . well, I can have it. . . . My advice to every young fellow that can afford it is . . . marry young.

In the text of *Stephen Hero*, Mr. Tobin of the Epiphany becomes Mr. Garvey. And here we have a clue which might lead to the identification of Garvey, who was really Tobin. Michael Tobin was a well-known reporter of strong nationalist feeling who later worked on *The Freeman's Journal*. Because of his involvement in the agrarian agitation of the time, he reported on Land League and other 'land for the people' meetings all over the country. Once he attended such a meeting at Doneraile, and not being satisfied with the quality of the speeches, decided it was an ideal opportunity to make one himself. He wired the text of his own speech back to head office, and had his own views on the 'state of the nation' put before the reading public the following day.

An entry in the Marriage Register of the Cathedral of Christ the King, Mullingar, for 10 October 1899, reads: 'Michael Tobin, Mullingar, son of Patrick Tobin, Doneraile, Cork, married Mary Hayden, Mullingar, daughter of Luke Hayden, Roscommon.' So, Mr. Tobin, *alias* Garvey, married *into* the *Westmeath Examiner*!

22 April 1899. Westmeath County Council.
Letter from Press.
Having from time to time to discharge onerous duties in the Court House of Mullingar, We, the journalists, representing the Press of Westmeath, and on behalf of our colleagues on the Dublin Press, desire to call the attention of the Council to the inadequate facilities which are placed at our disposal; this is characteristic of every department and an improved

arrangement is very much called for in this respect, particularly on all future occasions when the representatives of the people will be called upon to attend to important business, an amount of which the public will be so anxious to read. We would be glad to lay our views before a Committee or any of the Officials.

Signed: John P. Hayden
McDermott Hayes
Michael Tobin
John S. Hendrick.

It would appear that when James Joyce's father was preparing the voters' list he had access to the baptismal and marriage registers in the Cathedral in Mullingar and that his son accompanied him during the research. Because of this we find a clue as to why Joyce chose Garvey to replace Tobin in the text of *Stephen Hero*. At the christening of Michael Garvey's daughter, Elizabeth, born 1 November 1882, (Joyce's year of birth, and this date never failed to attract him), one of the sponsors was Norah Franklin, who later married Thomas Tobin of Celbridge. The name Nash often appears in the same pages, and a draper of this name lived opposite the 'Druggist's' in the main street of the town of Mullingar where the scene with the blind beggar took place.

Heffernan and Coughlan appear together as the contracting parties in a wedding, and the names Tate and Starkie are also found. But Mr. Tate's real name was George Stanislaus Dempsey, (Ellmann, *James Joyce*, p. 36). A family named Howard lived close to Lough Owel; in religion they were Dippers, which might explain the author's reference to Miss Howard's interest in the 'three kinds of baptism'.

Michael Tobin's 'partiality' to pig's crubeens was well known to his fellow journalists, and his carrying of them in his pocket often led him into trouble with hungry dogs, a fact which may have influenced Joyce's use of a similar incident in *Ulysses*.

Page 219: Garvey now decides on an even more delicate course, that of writing. On hearing from Nash that Stephen is inclined towards writing, his tip to the budding young author is very much to the point — shorthand! From a man who once got a 'par' into a London morning paper and got paid for it by return post, this is valuable indeed. Joyce at this time was already writing 'pars' for many papers.

At this point in the narrative the party has arrived at Anna Brook — here the Brosna river crosses under the street and flows on to collect the sewage of the Court House and jail before finally departing for Lough Ennell. Sweet Anna Brook had aroused many local poets to nostalgic elegies, as Anna Livia inspired Joyce years later, but the local rhymers flatter:

> Gliding 'round the ancient mill
>   Its crumbling walls, its wheel so still,
> O'er stepping stones you skip with ease
>   When passing through the ould Cross Keys,
> Twining through sweet Anna Brook,
>   Among flowery dell and shaded nook,
> And softly murmuring, on you sped,
>   By resting place of the honoured dead.

Flowery dells and shaded nooks appear to have little attraction for the trio, not even for the dog, and it is possible that the sensitive nostrils of Stephen were yet again assaulted by the stench of the sewage-laden Brosna, twining through 'sweet Anna Brook'.

In the *Twelfth Century Life of St. Colman of Lynn*, there is a reference to the Brosna which would have interested Joyce:

> The little boy who was nine months in my womb
> has endured many hours in the bright Brusna!

STEPHEN HERO

Cape, 253]

then what did we do but I thought if we could only get the lend of a pole off someone. So Joe and me, then, went down to the back of Slater's yard . . .

A pace or two from the brink of the water a thing was lying on the bank partly covered by a brown sack. It was the body of a woman: the face was to the ground and from the thick black hair a pool of water had oozed out. The body was curved upwards with legs abroad but over [word torn away] someone had drawn down the [word torn away] nightdress. The woman had escaped from the asylum the night before and Stephen heard many criticisms of the nurses.

— It'd be better for 'em mind the patients than traipsing about with every Tom, Dick and Harry of a doctor.

— It's them has the style.

Mr Garvey's dog wanted to sniff the body but Mr Garvey kicked him heavily and the dog curled up yelping. Then there was silence for some time, everyone remaining at his post watching the corpse, until a voice said 'Here's the doctor!' A stout well-dressed man came down the path quickly without acknowledging the salutes of the people and after a few moments Stephen heard him saying the woman was dead and telling the people to get a cart and have the body taken away. The three young men then continued their walk but Stephen had to be waited for and called to. He remained behind gazing into the canal near the feet of the body, looking at a fragment of paper on which was

ms. 506]

printed: The Lamp, a [mazn] magazine for . . . the rest was torn away and several other pieces of paper were floating about in the water.

The afternoon was well advanced before the young men separated. Stephen bade his friends goodbye, promising to renew acquaintance very soon, and took a path through the fields. The ground was very treacherous and he slipped often into bog-water. However he found a broad highway over the bog and here he was as secure as on the road. The sun was declining and against the deep gold of the western sky the figures of some bending turf-cutters were outlined. He reached Mr. Fulham's house by a back road and climbing over the fence came up through a little wood. As he walked on the soft grass he made no noise. At the edge of the wood he stood still. Miss Howard was leaning on the high painted gate facing the sunset. The full glow of the sunset had covered her sombre vesture with streaks of rust and scattered spangles of rust upon her sombre hair. Stephen came towards her but when he was a few paces

Cape, 253] They walk on, and when they come to the canal bridge they notice the crowd of people collected about fifty yards along the canal bank. The body of a middle-aged woman has been taken from the water, and lies on the margin. At this point the narrative assumes a frightening realism, revealing an obsession with death which haunted the author all his life. The added fact that the victim had been a patient in the Mullingar District Lunatic Asylum (as it was then called), seems a grim foreshadowing of the sad fate in store for Joyce's own daughter, Lucia, and his constant fear for her safety.

The incident is fully reported in the *Westmeath Guardian* of 20 July 1900, and in the hospital records. The findings of the inquest were direct:

> We find that the deceased, aged about 52 years, was drowned in the Royal Canal on the morning of the 19th July (1900), having escaped from the asylum on the same morning (3.30 a.m.), but we have not sufficient evidence as to how she escaped. Mr. Brophil, sworn juror, dissented, saying it should be: "we are not satisfied with the evidence as to how she escaped."

The verdict, however, was unanimously adopted.

The hospital records state, as the result of a sworn inquiry into the matter:

> Your Committee have considered the forcible comments in the Report of the Inspectors, touching on the death of the deceased, arising indirectly from the overcrowding on the female side of the main block. Your Committee believe that when the new chronic block is occupied, the temporary block will be vacated, thus affording accommodation for 75 patients. Your Committee think that the temporary block should be used for female accommodation. Your Committee is glad to see that the result of the judicial inquiry into the cause of death exonerates the entire staff.

Discussing the notorious 'Ball' held at the mental hospital in the autumn of 1901, Rev. E. O'Reilly, chaplain, and member of the board, referred to the expression used by Mr. Flynn with respect to the 'Ball', which he described as a 'saturnalia of immorality'. The board decided, however, that the reports were wild exaggerations, and commended the Resident Medical Superintendent, Dr. Arthur Finnegan, on the conduct of his staff.

It may be worth noticing that the young man who first saw the body 'went for Joe Coghlan' to help him pull the corpse from the water. In *Ulysses* we learn from Milly that the proprietor of the photographic shop in Mullingar is Mr. Coghlan.

And so, the nurses, who according to local gossip recorded by Stephen were 'traipsing about with every Tom, Dick and Harry of a doctor instead of minding their patients', were exonerated.

Joyce's description of the grotesque body clad only in a nightdress, the desire of Mr. Garvey's dog to sniff the body, and the reward the dog received for his canine inquisitiveness set a foreboding atmosphere in the sultry quietness of the summer's day. It is an almost overpowering image of tragic death, and the arrival of the doctor brings a welcome relief.

There is no mistaking this brusque, stout personality who ignores the saluting crowd — he is Doctor Dillon Kelly, a popular figure, a man who involved himself completely in the social, political and medical welfare of the town's people. He pronounces that the woman is dead, and with the detachment which is apparent on all such occasions, orders a cart to have the body taken away.

It is noticeable that Stephen is reluctant to leave the scene. He remains, gazing into the canal near the feet of the body, looking at a fragment of paper on which was printed, The Lamp.

ms. 506] *The Lamp, A Weekly Magazine for the Catholic Home*, consisted of twenty pages and cost one penny. It was published at 16 Bear Alley, Farringdon Street, London, and was already established for three-quarters of a century in 1900. Apart from the usual contents such as household notes, romantic serials and educational tit-bits, the magazine also devoted a section to short biographical essays, usually illustrated with a portrait, of some notable Irish writers of the day. The 1900 issues featured amongst others, William O'Brien, Mr. Justin McCarthy, M.P., Reminiscences of Daniel O'Connell by his granddaughter, Alice O'Connell, and Sir Charles Gavan Duffy. In all of the issues for the year 1900, an editorial note advises: 'The Editor of *The Lamp* has now on hand an ample supply of accepted manuscripts, and is unable to consider any further contributions in the meantime.'

It seemed that for budding authors, *The Lamp* was, for the time being, a closed shop; but to its extensive readership it offered a miscellany of contributions which knew no bounds. One could read of St. Rita of Casola, or of Pope Leo's humour; that stammering men are four times as numerous as stammering women, and that blue-eyed people are seldom colour-blind. In the issue of 23 July 1900, a note headed '*The Value of a Wife's Sympathy*' must have been read with great approval, and might even have drawn Joyce's attention: 'Solicitude and disappointment enter the history of every man's life, and he is but half provided for his voyage who finds an associate only for happy hours, while for his months of darkness and distress no sympathizing partner is prepared.'

It would have been ironic if the unfortunate woman who had strayed into the canal in the 'darkest hours' of that July morning had been holding that copy of *The Lamp* in her hand as she drowned; the same pages perhaps which later floated at the feet of her corpse.

* * *

Having said farewell to his friends, Nash and Garvey, Stephen heads for home across the bog. In this passage as in many others of James Joyce there are echoes of Synge: 'the deep gold of the Western sky' and 'the bending turf-cutters'. In *A Portrait of the Artist* we read of the girl standing alone in the rivulet in the strand — 'the likeness of a strange and beautiful seabird' — 'long slender bare legs were delicate as a crane's' (*A Portrait*, p. 195).

This description may be compared to that written by Synge in a similar setting:

> I often come on a girl with her petticoats tucked up round her, standing in a pool left by the tide and washing her flannels among the sea-anemones and crabs. Their red bodices and white tapering legs make them as beautiful as tropical sea-birds, as they stand in a frame of seaweeds against the brink of the Atlantic.
> (*The Aran Islands,* Oxford University Press, The World's Classics, 1967, pp. 193-194.)

Buck Mulligan's warning to Stephen that the tramper Synge was out in pampooties to murder him for pissing on his halldoor in Glasthule, and perhaps worse still, parodying his 'mister honey', and his 'droughty clerics', may have had more than the 'gleeful' foundation recorded so hilariously in *Ulysses*. (p. 188)

Having survived the treacherous bog-holes, Stephen arrives home at Mr. Fulham's house by a back road. Noiselessly he comes upon a scene which stops him in his tracks. Miss Howard is leaning on a high, painted gate facing the sunset. . . . Stephen comes towards her 'but when he was a few paces. . . .'

At this tantalizing moment the manuscript pages end. Miss Howard stands in the sunset glow, transformed by the 'deep gold of the western sky'. For Stephen it is a climactic moment of experience, maybe his first experience of what the author later described as 'inexpressible love' . . . 'crying to greet the advent of the life that had cried to him' (*A Portrait*, p. 196).

During the writing of these pages of *Stephen Hero* James Joyce was undergoing perhaps the most crucial years of his life. It was the eve of his departure from Church and country—of renouncing the world for his art, yet soon assuming the responsibility of a wife and family. The author's own admission sums up the situation best: 'It must be said simply and at once that at this time Stephen suffered the most enduring influence of his life.' (*Stephen Hero*, p. 45.) Here, according to one Joyce scholar, 'the author is not merely reporting a fact concerning his character, but also, by strident emphasis, announcing his own position.'

'. . . As already indicated, *Stephen Hero* not only elucidates passages in Joyce's other works; it also prefigures Joyce's later activity, in particular his development as a craftsman. . . .' (Joseph Prescott, *James Joyce's Stephen Hero*, The English Literature Society, Korea University.)

Milly Bloom and the photographer's shop

The second or 'reflective' stage of the *Mullingar Connection* carries us into the writing of *Ulysses* and *Finnegans Wake*. The best known link is, of course, Milly Bloom and the photographer's shop in Mullingar. Richard Ellmann in his definitive biography, *James Joyce*, records his reasons why the photographer's shop was located in Mullingar, on the strength of an interview given to him by the late Brinsley MacNamara in 1954.

> Joyce no doubt also knew of another Bloom, who was committed in Wexford early in the century for the murder of a girl who worked with him in a photographer's shop. He had planned a double suicide; after having killed her and, as he thought, himself, he scrawled the word LOVE (but misspelt it as LIOVE) with his blood on the wall behind him. He was let off on mental grounds and, after some time in an institution, left the country. This incident presumably gave Joyce the plan of establishing Bloom's daughter Milly as an apprentice in a photographer's shop. He put the shop in Mullingar because he remembered that there was such a shop there when he visited the town with his father in 1900 and 1901. (Ellmann, *James Joyce*, p. 386.)

But we find other reasons in Molly Bloom's soliloquy, reasons which strengthen yet further the Mullingar Connection:

> ... still its the feeling, especially now with Milly away, such an idea for him to send the girl down there to learn to take photographs on account of his grandfather instead of sending her to Skerrys academy where she'd have to learn. ... (*Ulysses*, p. 725.)

Before the 15th anniversary of her birth (*Ulysses*, p. 654), Milly Bloom was sent to Mullingar to work in Phil Shaw's photographic establishment as an apprentice (Ellmann, *James Joyce*, p. 386). Milly was sent to Mullingar because she was getting out of bounds in Dublin, 'riding Harry Devan's bike at night in Nelson Street, and smoking cigarettes in the skating rink' (*Ulysses*, p. 726).

These misdemeanours of Milly's hardly compare acrobatically with Isabel's in *Finnegans Wake*, (p. 270, 23-24), who is freewheeling 'on Youthlits bilke' with her feet on the 'algebrars'.

Stephen hears Malachi's gossip of the holidaying down in Westmeath and how Bannon has found 'a sweet young thing down there. Photo girl he calls her'. (*Ulysses*, p. 19.) Milly writes to her father, mentioning a Mr. Coghlan for whom she works, and also mentions the young student, Bannon. (*Ulysses*, p. 54.) Later, we have the actual letter in full in which Milly, after the usual thanks for the presents from home, reveals that the shop is busy, especially on fair days. She tells of the proposed picnic on Lough Owel, the coming concert in the *Greville Arms*, and then after a mention of the student Bannon, who has been down in Mullingar and has returned to Dublin, she closes the letter with fondest love to her Papli. Like many fond daughters she also excuses the bad writing and the hurry. (*Ulysses*, pp. 58-59).

Bloom recalls this letter affectionately as he considers his dear girl, who will soon be a woman (*Ulysses*, p. 81).

As Paddy Dignam's funeral crosses the Royal Canal at Crossguns bridge, Bloom recalls the eastward journey from Athlone to Dublin aboard the famous canal boat, the *Bugabu*. He contemplates going to see Milly 'by canal, or cycle down' (*Ulysses*, p. 91). Bloom remembers 'Milly as a kiddy' when crossing Westmoreland Street, recalling happy days.

> Happy. Happier then. Snug little room that was with the red wallpaper, Dockrell's, one-and-ninepence a dozen. Milly's tubbing night. American soap I bought: elderflower. Cosy smell of her bathwater. Funny she looked soaped all over. Shapely too. Now photography. Poor Papa's daguerreotype atelier he told me of. Hereditary taste. (*Ulysses*, p. 144.)

Leopold Bloom's cousin, Stefan Virag of Szesfehervar, Hungary, was a photographer, and the executor of the 'daguerreotype' referred to here. 'An indistinct daguerreotype of Rudolph Virag and his father Leopold Virag executed in the year 1852 in the portrait atelier of their (respectively) 1st and 2nd cousin, Stefan Virag of Szesfehervar, Hungary.' (*Ulysses*, p. 684.)

It may be worth recording in reference to 'Papa's daguerreotype', that the Italian name for a photographer is 'Papparazzi', a fact well known to James Joyce.

Mrs. Breen interrupts the 'Happy Happy' reverie by enquiring after Molly. Bloom informs her that Molly is 'in the pink' and that Milly has a position down in Mullingar, in a photographer's, and that she is 'getting on like a house on fire' (*Ulysses*, p. 145).

Outside the Rt. Hon. Mr. Justice Fitzgibbon's door in Holles Street, Malachi and Alec Bannon discuss Milly — they speak of her as a 'skittish heifer, big of her age and beef to the heel' (*Ulysses*, p. 379).

In Holles Street Maternity Hospital, Malachi Mulligan appears in the doorway, accompanied by his friend, Alec Bannon, who had late come to town (*Ulysses*, p. 384). Bannon, speaking of his affair with Milly, mentions her as the 'bold bad girl from the town of Mullingar' (*Ulysses*, p. 407).

The last meeting with Milly is a rather startling one — in Nighttown. Here she is in the arms of the Mullingar student, who is now her lover. Wearing a green dress with her hair dyed gold, she is mistakenly recognized by Bloom as Molly until Bello mockingly tells him that she is his daughter Milly (*Ulysses*, p. 514).

Joyce does not mention the photographic shop in the 'Mullingar pages' of *Stephen Hero*, which is a strange omission, but then only half the original manuscript of more than a thousand pages was preserved.

Photography played an important part in the reveries of Leopold Bloom, and in the early life of his daughter, Milly. Was this interest because of, as Bloom himself says 'Hereditary taste', or was it something more personal in the author's own life which guided Milly into the photographer's shop in Mullingar? Which leads us to another very interesting speculation: that in the creation of Milly Bloom and her Mullingar lover, Joyce sought to avenge himself on a town which, it seems, kept him at arm's length. Until some more pages of *Stephen Hero* are discovered, the answer remains hidden away; an unrevealed secret of the enigmatic and dignified Miss Howard (still) standing at the garden gate in the gold of the evening sun. Or perhaps an even more fragile ever-fading image on an exposed film in Milly Bloom's camera, exposed, but forever awaiting development.

... Finiche! only a fadograph of a yestern scene ...

The Earl Street Post Office, which later came under the management of Phil Shaw, is shown on maps of the early nineteenth century. The photographic and stationery business was well established at the turn of the century as the following advertisement shows:

21 July 1900
Photography — I will be in all parts of Westmeath during the year, taking photographs for a publishing firm. If you want anything photographed, please drop me a card, and I will let you know the day I will be in your neighbourhood.
Phil Shaw, Earl Street P.O., Mullingar.

23 March 1901
Phil Shaw now has the largest stock in town of Rosary Beads, Prayer Books, Statues, Scapulars, Religious Pictures and Books.
Habits at 5/-, 7/6 and 10/6.

It is interesting to speculate on the 'bold bad girl from the town of Mullingar', dreaming away the hours in the photographic darkroom or fondling the religious objects or an occasional habit! Perhaps her thoughts may have strayed to the ancient churchyard at Portloman, on the shores of Lough Owel, where, even to the present day may be seen the name of 'Bannon' carved on the trees, and where the 'picnic' mentioned in her letter to her father may have taken place.

Lomman Locha Uair — St. Lomman of Lough Owel, was a descendant of Niall of the Nine Hostages, High King of Ireland, who died in 405 A.D. The western shores of Lough Owel, near the hills of Slanemore and Frewin, were the scene of the bloody battles between the Leinstermen and the grandsons of Niall of the Nine Hostages. In 515 A.D. the warlike invaders finally triumphed, and the plains of Meath, in area approximating to the present Diocese of Meath, were seized and afterwards called the 'Kingdom of Meath'.

From these invaders, Lomman of Lough Owel was sprung, and on the western shores of the lake, near the foot of Frewin Hill, he was born in 657 A.D. Very little is known of him, but tradition records that he was born, lived and died there. In the memory of the people, even to the present day, it is doubtful if any other Irish saint is so vividly remembered and loved as Lomman of Lough Owel.

One time there was a terrible plague in Ireland and when it spread to this part of the country the people were afraid for their lives, and they went to Lomman and asked him to save them. So Lomman yoked his plough and he ploughed a furrow all round the parish of Portlomman, and nobody died of the plague inside that furrow nor did anyone die of any plague since. Ever since Lomman did that, nobody ever begins the spring ploughing till after the feastday of the Saint on the 7th of February.

Within a mile of Portloman, in a westerly direction, is the hill of Slanemore — the Slemain of the ancient tale — the *Táin Bó Cuailnge*. Here, it is said, the Ultonians encamped when pursuing Queen Medb and her army after the celebrated raid into Ulster. There are three mounds on the hill said to have been erected by Conor Mac Nessa's army. One of the mounds, which is very much larger than the other two, is, perhaps, the one referred to in the *Táin*.

The Lakes Ennell and Owel are named after two Firbolgian princes, Ainninn and Uair.

Ainninn and Uair were two sons of the Kings of the Firbolg. And as regards pedigree they were of the men of the Greeks. And the Greeks prevailed upon them and deprived them of their sweet tasted water, and the Firbolg were made subject to slavery, namely, to drag mould onto bare stones. So they fled before the tyranny to Ireland and they did not set up there except near clear watered lakes. So Ainninn and Uair set up at two of them that were equal, north and south, and there they both died, each at his lake. And from them the lakes are named Loch Ainninn and Loch

Uair. (From the *Dinnseanchus — The Placenames of Westmeath*, Fr. Paul Walsh.)

The 'Modder ilond' diagram in *Finnegans Wake*, p. 293, and the pages leading up to, and following, it seem to have special historical and archaeological references to Lough Ennell and Uisneagh Hill, which are situated a few miles from each other in Westmeath. The area within the boundaries of Lough Ennell and Uisneagh was an ancient sub-division of *Cenel Fiachach*, or Keneleagh, named *Kinel Enda*.

Lough Owel, also called Lough Foyle and Lough Hoyle, is according to an unusual legend, the lake of the borrowed water. The legend relates that two sisters lived, one in Westmeath and one in Roscommon. The former asked for, and got, the loan of the water which lay in County Roscommon where the track of the lake bed is still pointed out. The term of the contract was 'till Monday', but the Westmeath lass altered it to 'the Monday after eternity', and the borrowed lake was never returned.

The sudden storms which sometimes ruffle the water of Lough Owel are said to be caused by the anger of the Roscommon sister who frequently visits the lake, demanding return of the waters which she delivered in good faith, and which have now gone from her grasp forever.

The great Viking leader, Turgeis, plundered the surrounding counties from bases in the midland lakes. In 845 A.D., Malachy I, King of Meath, captured Turgeis and drowned him in Lough Owel. Soudare Island, or more correctly 'Soudari', Soudar, the Danish word for south, and I, the word for an island — South Island, bears witness to the Viking occupation of Lough Owel. The Captain's Hill, on the eastern shore of the lake, has a burial mound which may be the resting place of the warrior Turgeis. A fitting burial, perhaps, when one remembers that it was from the said hill that Turgeis was thrown by Malachy to his death.

The name Turgeis is not found in the English or Scandinavian records of the Vikings. On the other hand the *Irish Annals* make no mention of Regnar Lodbrog who, according to the *Danish Chronicles*, was killed in Ireland. It is surmised that Turgeis (servant or worshipper of Thor) was in fact Regnor Lodbrog, a king of Denmark, who spent most of his time campaigning abroad. Regnor Lodbrok's snake-proof pants are worn by H.C.E. in one of the Prankquean stories in *Finnegans Wake*.

James Joyce became interested in the Rochfort family through their association with Belvedere College, which had originally been built as a residence for George Rochfort, second Earl of Belvedere, in 1786. It was Joyce's ambition to make a contribution to Irish history by writing the tragic story of Lady Belvedere and her lover (Ellmann, *James Joyce*, p. 245). A lengthy version of this story first appeared in *The Edinburgh Review* in 1846, and was later printed by the author, J. C. Lyons, in his famous book, *Grand Juries of Westmeath*. Almost one hundred years had then elapsed since Mary, wife of Robert Rochfort, first Earl of Belvedere, had suffered a conjugal imprisonment of thirty years for supposed adultery with her husband's younger brother, Arthur. Part of the evidence produced at the trial was a series of very incriminating love letters between the parties, but the letters were never fully proven and later were considered as forgeries.

The unfortunate Countess, on the advice of her friends, pleaded guilty, having been assured that such action would end in divorce and release from her vengeful husband. But the co-respondent, Arthur Rochfort, fearful for the safety of his own wife and family, had fled the country, and the result of the trial was the granting of a separation but not a divorce.

The frustrated Earl imprisoned his wife in Gaulstown House, where she remained a captive from 1743 until the Earl's death in 1774.

Gaulstown House had no longer any attraction for the Earl and he built a magnificent lodge on the shores of Lough Ennell, about six miles from his seat. Here he lived sumptuously, and according to some accounts lecherously, paying occasional visits to Gaulstown, but avoiding any contact with his captive wife. It is said that the servant who accompanied Mary Rochfort on her recreational walks through the gardens carried a warning bell which was rung continuously to guard against accidental confrontations.

George Rochfort, Earl of Bellfield, and younger brother of Robert, had played a large part in sowing the seeds of intrigue and suspicion which had resulted in the downfall of Countess Mary. During the early years of Robert's marriage, George had been an adviser and confidant of the Earl, but the progress of years changed their relationship. When the Earl was building Belvedere Lodge, George was building a much more magnificent house within view of it, and a serious rivalry sprang up between the brothers.

Sir James Caldwell of Castle Caldwell, visited both houses in 1773 and described the contrasting ways of life:

> At Rochfort, home of George, Lord Bellfield, all was regularity and religion, but at Belvedere, all was debauchery and dissipation.

Earlier, the jealous Earl had a large castellated folly erected between the houses to obstruct the view of one from the other. This folly, since called the 'jealous wall', still stands as a grim reminder of the paranoic mind attempting to hide its guilt from the eyes of the world.

Mary Rochfort was truly a tragic figure, and in her moment of trial was disowned by her father, Lord Molesworth, as a bastard daughter. Before her marriage at the tender age of 16 years, she seems to have had a premonition of her future disastrous life. She had made her theatrical debut at one of Lord Mountjoy's private theatricals, playing a part in *The Distressed Mother*. She also had her portrait painted in the style of another famous captive, Mary, Queen of Scots.

In *Ulysses* we read of Mary, first Countess of Belvedere, walking the shores of Lough Ennel listlessly — an image recollected by Father Conmee as he thinks of his little book, *Old Times in the Barony*. The theme of cuckoldry is also echoed in Stephen's theory that Shakespeare was cuckolded by his brothers.

Joyce may have been surprised to discover that the association of Mary Belvedere and Lough Ennell was incorrect, and that the Countess had never lived at Belvedere House (Ellmann, *James Joyce*, p. 761, note 62). He never proceeded with his stated intention of writing the story of Lord and Lady Belvedere, maybe because he decided Mary was a figure of tragedy rather than guilt.

Old Times in the Barony (*Ulysses*, p. 222), by Very Rev. J. S. Conmee, S.J., was originally published in *The New Ireland Review* in Dublin in January 1895, under the pseudonym, Max Wood, a name probably adopted from Fr. Mac's Wood at Clongowes. A reprint of the work was published by the Catholic Truth Society of Ireland in 1900 (N. W. English, Athlone).

A Brilliant Career

Yet another link in the Mullingar connection is Joyce's first play, *A Brilliant Career*, which, according to Stanislaus Joyce, was completed there in July, 1900. The story of the triangular association, Joyce—Ibsen—Mullingar, begins in the previous January when, having overcome what he interpreted as attempted censorship by Father Delaney, President of the College Literary and Historical Society, Joyce was permitted to read his paper 'Drama and Life' in the Physics Theatre, University College, Dublin. After the reading, having listened to a well organized barrage of criticism, he defended his position, mentioning the immense importance of Ibsen's social themes, the importance of the artist in the community, and that drama was in itself the highest form of art. He spoke for thirty minutes, answering all the points, without once referring to notes.

It seems certain that *A Brilliant Career* was begun and completed in Mullingar during the month of July, 1900, but the mere accident of geographical composition might not forge any link between Joyce and Mullingar were it not for the parallel conditions then existing in the town.

On 1 April of the same year that select journal, *The Fortnightly Review*, published an article by Joyce on Ibsen's play, *When We Dead Awaken*; for which Joyce received a twelve guinea reward.

In a letter to William Archer dated 16 April, Ibsen complimented Joyce on the article, and on 23 April Archer relayed the praises to Joyce, mentioning Ibsen's apology that his knowledge of the language in which the article was written did not permit him to make personal thanks.

Joyce replied to Archer on 28 April, thanking him for his letter and assuring him that he would keep Ibsen in his heart all his life. In May of that year, Joyce called on Archer in London where they dined together, but no promise was made of a future meeting.

He dedicated the play in an extraordinary manner, particularly so as it was the only work he was ever to dedicate. On the dedicatory page was written:

<blockquote>
To
My Own Soul I
dedicate the first
true work of my
life
</blockquote>

In the story of *A Brilliant Career*, a young doctor, torn between his love for a woman and his ambition for success decides to marry a different woman who furthers his career and enables him to become mayor of the town.

Because of sewage problems in the town a plague breaks out, and the mayor finds himself aided in combating the pestilence by an unknown woman, who turns out to be Angela, the one he has betrayed. She is now married to a jealous husband. The brilliant career loses some of its brilliance as the mayor and the betrayed wife say farewell in an atmosphere of bitterness.

Joyce, at this time and for a few years later, was contemplating a medical career, but after brief studies in Paris and Dublin he dropped the idea. (Ellmann, *James Joyce*, pp. 72-83.)

During the writing of *A Brilliant Career*, Mullingar was having its own problems with the Ibsenite themes described best by William Archer in a letter to Joyce as 'A huge fable of politics and pestilence' (Ellmann, *James Joyce*, p. 82. Letter from William Archer to James Joyce, 15 September 1900). The problems of Ibsen's Dr. Stockmann in *An Enemy of the People*, Joyce's doctor in *A Brilliant Career*, and Dr. Edgar Flynn of the Local Government Board had a startling similarity. The situation is described by Dr. Flynn in his report as Medical Inspector.

Letter No. 25324, 5 May 1900, from Local Government Board forwarding copy of a report which they had received from their Medical Inspector, Dr. Edgar Flynn, relative to the drainage and sewerage of the town of Mullingar.

Copy of report.
Mullingar Rural District Council.
I recently visited Mullingar in reference to the question of the sewerage and drainage of the town — there can be no doubt but that the whole of the system at present in existence is very insanitary and a danger to the health of the inhabitants. A considerable percentage of the drainage from dwelling-houses discharges into surface drains on the public thoroughfares. The river Brosna, which flows through the town, receives practically all the sewerage, and in its course through Mullingar partakes of the character of an open sewer, and at some places a most offensive odour is emitted. This river, being comparatively small and narrow, its pollution becomes very evident. Until a proper system of main drainage is carried out, it will be impossible to devise a method to prevent the pollution of this river. Of the necessity of such a system there can be no doubt, but in view of the fact that a scheme of water supply is about to be provided for the town, it would seem judicious to await its introduction, as the question of a system of main drainage can be better approached and devised. A great improvement can, however, be effected in the conditions of the surface drains on the principal thoroughfare, the drainage from which ultimately finds its way into the River Brosna. The surface water in these drains, mixed as it is with organic and vegetable refuse matter, remains stagnant, and gives off most offensive odours. There can be no difficulty in devising a system of daily cleansing and

flushing of these drains, and more careful attention should be given to the question of public cleansing and scavenging in the principal thoroughfares where these drains are situated. At present the insanitary condition of these drains is a danger and a menace to the public health of the town.

Dr. Edgar Flynn
27 April 1900

Joyce sent the play to Archer on 30 August, when the family had already left Mullingar and returned to Dublin, and on 15 September had a long, critical, but favourable reply. Archer assured him that he had talent, more than talent, but that the play was not fully successful. He summed up his feelings at the end of the letter by again assuring Joyce of his interest, and his desire to read any further work of a dramatic nature.

He returned the manuscript, and Joyce wrote, thanking him for his criticism. Two years later Joyce destroyed the play; all that remains are four lines of a gypsy song sung in a merrymaking scene. Besides the prose play, he wrote one in verse entitled *Dream Stuff*; only one stanza from a song remains (Ellmann, *James Joyce*, p. 83).

During the summer of 1901, which Joyce also spent with his father in Mullingar, he translated two of Hauptmann's plays. The first, *Vor Sonnenaufgang* (*Before Sunrise*), was the play which made Hauptmann famous a dozen years before, while *Michael Kramer* was Hauptmann's most recent work (1900) (Ellmann, *James Joyce*, p. 91).

The translation of Hauptmann's *Michael Kramer* reappears in the writing desk of Mr. James Duffy of 'A Painful Case' in Joyce's *Dubliners*.

In both these Mullingar summers Joyce was preparing voluminous notes for *Stephen Hero*, which he later took with him to Paris.

Epilogue

And now a last 'aside' . . . not a resounding finale, maybe only a 'treestirm shindy' or a 'shandy westerness', but on a happy note, 'joy with a shandy' even if 'rather sternish'.

Laurence Sterne, mentioned many times in *Finnegans Wake*, had a street named after a relation of his in Mullingar: Sterne Street. He lived in the town about the year 1722. He writes:

> We all decamped (from Wicklow, where his father, an army officer, was stationed) but got no further than Droheda, thence ordered to Mullingar, forty miles west, where by providence we stumbled upon a kind relation, a colateral descendent of Archbishop Sterne, who took us to his castle and kindly treated us for a year, and sent us to the regiment in Carrickmacross loaded with kindnesses etc. . . A most rueful and tedious journey had we all, in March, to Carrickfergus where we arrived in six or seven days.

The houses on Sterne Street were demolished about 1825 to make room for the building of the new courthouse and jail. Sterne Street was renamed Jail Street, and is to-day called Seery Street after Bryan Seery who was hanged in Mullingar in 1846 for an assault on the person of Sir Francis Hopkins. The main evidence against Seery was that a hat found at the scene of the crime fitted him.

There is a constant play on the title of Laurence Sterne's famous novel, *Tristram Shandy*, in *Finnegans Wake*.

Tristram Shandy, being a voice *in Utero* so to speak, would naturally be given a sympathetic hearing in Holles Street Hospital. It is understandable that Joyce found it convenient and appropriate to resort to the style of Laurence Sterne in these surroundings, but it is interesting to note that it is the appearance of Alec Bannon, Milly's lover from the town of Mullingar, which marks the change to this style. One might assume, and perhaps with justification, that the Mullingar arrival prompted Joyce to resort to the style of *Tristram Shandy* because of Laurence Sterne's association with the town which named a street after him.

Also worthy of notice is the declaration by H. G. Wells in his review of *A Portrait* written for *The Nation*, 24 February 1917, that Sterne himself could not have done the Christmas Dinner better. (Ellmann, *James Joyce*, p. 427.)

The Christmas Dinner scene might well have been recorded verbatim in Mullingar during Joyce's stay there; a fact easily verified from the columns of local newspapers of the time, and so perhaps yet another link in the connection is forged.

Asides, those interesting theatrical relics, could hardly ever satisfactorily substitute for epilogues. But there is no real reason why the epilogue should not also take the form of an aside, and so this final word is offered in the manner of that which has already been said.

It is hardly necessary to recall the political themes or the characters who donned the masks to exploit them during Joyce's stay in Mullingar in the first summers of the twentieth century. Everywhere in the country, then, there were messianic figures playing, yes, the Parnell role; for some it was difficult to accept that their chief had really died. Also noticeable was the paradoxical situation that what was known as, yes, the Parnell struggle was much more alive and vibrant after his death than ever during his lifetime. Certain sections of the Mullingar community were being constantly reminded of this situation by bitter accusations. Joyce himself was a victim of the same strange phenomenon of Irish society, if indeed it is a phenomenon and not an inevitability.

Apart altogether from the political nuances of the era, other questions arise which one must answer for oneself. Were the impressions and recollections which guided H.C.E. to the Mullingar Inn at Chapelizod related to those which ushered Milly Bloom into the photographer's shop in Mullingar and later, yes, into the arms of her Mullingar lover in Nighttown? Might we accept that the formative experience recorded by Stephen himself in *Stephen Hero* as 'the most enduring influence of his life' was so enduring as to survive the Trieste-Zürich-Paris exile of two score years? Considering the Mullingar connection as revealed in these few pages, dare one whisper an affirmative

yes

James Joyce and the Mullingar Connection by Leo Daly is the twentieth Dolmen Edition. The book, designed by Liam Miller and set in Times Roman type, has been seen through the press by Liam Browne and printed and published at the Dolmen Press, North Richmond Industrial Estate, North Richmond Street, Dublin 1, in the Republic of Ireland. Jim Hughes was the compositor and Garrett Doyle the pressman. This edition, which is for sale in the U.S.A. and in Canada only, is limited to 250 copies.

Leo Daly.

Humanities Press Inc.,
171 First Avenue,
Atlantic Highlands,
New Jersey 07716.